WeightW

Vegetarian recipes for family and friends

Meat-free Meals

SIMON & SCHUSTER ILLUSTRATED

London · New York · Sydney · Toronto · New Delhi

A CBS COMPANY

Weight Watchers **ProPoints** Weight Loss System is a simple way to lose weight. As part of the Weight Watchers **ProPoints** plan you'll enjoy eating delicious, healthy, filling foods that help to keep you feeling satisfied for longer and in control of your portions.

V This symbol denotes a vegetarian recipe and assumes that, where relevant, free range eggs, vegetarian cheese, vegetarian virtually fat free fromage frais, vegetarian low fat crème fraîche and vegetarian low fat yogurts are used. Virtually fat free fromage frais, low fat crème fraîche and low fat yogurts may contain traces of gelatine so they are not always vegetarian. Please check the labels.

❅ This symbol denotes a dish that can be frozen. Unless otherwise stated, you can freeze the finished dish for up to 3 months. Defrost thoroughly and reheat until the dish is piping hot throughout.

Recipe notes

Egg size: Medium, unless otherwise stated.

Raw eggs: Only the freshest eggs should be used. Pregnant women, the elderly and children should avoid recipes with eggs that are not fully cooked or raw.

All fruits and vegetables: Medium, unless otherwise stated.

Stock: Stock cubes are used in recipes, unless otherwise stated. These should be prepared according to packet instructions.

Recipe timings: These are approximate and meant to be guidelines. Please note that the preparation time includes all the steps up to and following the main cooking time(s).

Microwaves: Timings and temperatures are for a standard 800 W microwave. If necessary, adjust your own microwave.

Low fat spread: Where a recipe states to use a low fat spread, a light spread with a fat content of no less than 38% should be used.

Low fat soft cheese: Where low fat soft cheese is specified in a recipe, this refers to soft cheese with a fat content of less than 5%.

Contents

Introduction

Not just for vegetarians, *Meat-free Meals* is packed full of wonderful recipes that everyone will love. Making the most of seasonal vegetables, these fantastic recipes from the best of Weight Watchers cookbooks are perfect for all the family.

From light bites, such as a Grilled Aubergine Sandwich or Lunchbox Pea and Mint Frittatas, to supper dishes like Red Wine Mushrooms with Polenta Mash, Spinach and Potato Gratin or Vegetable Balti, there is something here for all occasions. So, whether you are vegetarian or just wanting to eat less meat, give these tasty recipes and try and surprise your family and friends with *Meat-free Meals*.

About Weight Watchers

For more than 40 years Weight Watchers has been helping people around the world to lose weight using a long term sustainable approach. Weight Watchers successful weight loss system is based on four tried and trusted principles:

- Eating healthily
- Being more active
- Adjusting behaviour to help weight loss
- Getting support in weekly meetings

Our unique *ProPoints* system empowers you to manage your food plan and make wise recipe choices for a healthier, happier you. To find out more about Weight Watchers and the *ProPoints* values for these recipes, contact Customer Services on 0845 345 1500.

Meat-free cooking

Vegetarian cooking is not just for people who don't eat meat, poultry or fish. Anyone can cook and enjoy meat-free meals, and you may find you enjoy these recipes so much you swap your old favourite meat dishes for some new vegetarian ones. Many vegetarians eat eggs and dairy products, and we have included recipes with these in this book. If you are a vegetarian and following a more restrictive diet, please check the recipes to see whether they contain eggs or dairy products.

Make the most of seasonal produce and don't be afraid to try new vegetables and flavours. By ringing the changes you'll be eating a greater variety of fruit and vegetables throughout the year and you'll be less likely to get bored with the same old ingredients.

Storing and freezing

Many dishes store well in the fridge, but make sure you use them up within a day or two. Some can also be frozen. However, it is important to make sure you freeze safely.

- Wrap any food to be frozen in rigid containers or strong freezer bags.
- Label the containers or bags with the contents and date.
- Never freeze warm food – always let it cool completely first.
- Never freeze food that has already been frozen and defrosted.
- Defrost what you need in the fridge.
- Most fruit and vegetables can be frozen by open freezing. Lay them out on a tray, freeze until solid and then pack them into bags.

- Some vegetables, such as peas, broccoli and broad beans can be blanched first by cooking for 2 minutes in boiling water. Drain, refresh under cold water and then freeze once cold. Vegetables with a high water content, such as salad leaves, cannot be frozen.
- Fresh herbs are great frozen – either seal leaves in bags or, for soft herbs such as basil and parsley, chop finely and add to ice cube trays with water. These are great for dropping into casseroles or soups straight from the freezer.

Shopping hints and tips

Always buy the best ingredients you can afford. If you are going to cook healthy meals, it is worth investing in some quality ingredients that will really add flavour to your dishes. Try a good quality olive oil and the best balsamic vinegar you can afford for dressings; avoid ready grated Parmesan and buy a block of the best you can find instead. Even changing staple foods like pasta and rice can increase flavour. Try imported dried pastas, which have a wheaty bread-like taste and will stay al dente better. Or swap plain white rice for brown basmati rice or jasmine rice and see the difference.

When you're going around the supermarket it's tempting to pick up foods you like and put them in your trolley without thinking about how you will use them. So, a good plan is to decide what dishes you want to cook before you go shopping, check your store cupboard and make a list of what you need.

We've added a checklist here for some of the store cupboard ingredients used in this book. Just add fresh ingredients in your regular shop and you'll be ready to cook the wonderful recipes in *Meat-free Meals*.

Store cupboard checklist

- [ ] apricots, canned in natural juice
- [ ] artichoke hearts, canned
- [ ] artificial sweetener
- [ ] bay leaves
- [ ] borlotti beans, canned
- [ ] bulgar wheat, dried
- [ ] butter beans, canned
- [ ] cayenne pepper
- [ ] chick peas, canned
- [ ] chilli (flakes and powder)
- [ ] chilli sauce
- [ ] Chinese five spice
- [ ] coconut milk, reduced fat
- [ ] cooking spray, calorie controlled
- [ ] coriander seeds
- [ ] coriander, ground
- [ ] cornflour
- [ ] couscous, dried
- [ ] cumin seeds
- [ ] cumin, ground
- [ ] curry (paste and powder)
- [ ] fennel seeds
- [ ] flour, plain

- [ ] gravy granules
- [ ] haricot beans, canned
- [ ] harissa paste
- [ ] herbs, dried (mixed and Italian)
- [ ] honey, runny
- [ ] horseradish sauce
- [ ] kidney beans, canned
- [ ] lentils, dried
- [ ] mushroom ketchup
- [ ] mushrooms, dried
- [ ] mustard (Dijon and wholegrain)
- [ ] mustard seeds
- [ ] noodles, dried
- [ ] oil, olive
- [ ] olives in brine, black
- [ ] paprika
- [ ] passata
- [ ] pasta, dried
- [ ] peppercorns
- [ ] peppers, piquante in a jar
- [ ] pesto sauce
- [ ] pineapple, canned in natural juice
- [ ] polenta, dried

- [ ] rice, dried (basmati and long grain)
- [ ] salt
- [ ] soy sauce
- [ ] stock cubes
- [ ] sugar, caster
- [ ] sweetcorn, canned
- [ ] Tabasco sauce
- [ ] tomato purée
- [ ] tomatoes, canned
- [ ] turmeric
- [ ] vinegar (balsamic and white wine)
- [ ] water chestnuts, canned

Soups and salads

Watercress and blue cheese soup

Serves 4
148 calories per serving
Takes 20 minutes
Ⓥ

25 g (1 oz) low fat spread

2 bunches of spring onions, chopped

300 g (10½ oz) potatoes, peeled and grated coarsely

850 ml (1½ pints) vegetable stock

85 g packet watercress

salt and freshly ground black pepper

50 g (1¾ oz) blue cheese, crumbled, to serve

A little blue cheese goes a long way in this recipe, with the crumbled cheese melting lusciously into the soup and boosting the flavour.

1 In a large, lidded, non stick saucepan, melt the low fat spread, add the spring onions and cook for 2 minutes until softened.

2 Add the potatoes and stock. Cover the pan and bring to the boil. Cook for 6–8 minutes until the potatoes are tender.

3 Stir the watercress into the soup, transfer to a blender, or use a hand held blender, and whizz until smooth. Return to the pan to reheat if necessary.

4 Check the seasoning and then ladle the soup into warmed bowls. Scatter the blue cheese over each bowl, to melt as you eat it.

Carrot and lentil soup

Serves 4
248 calories per serving
Takes 30 minutes
Ⓥ
❄

calorie controlled cooking
  spray
1 large onion, chopped
**1 celery stick with leaves,
  both sliced thinly**
**2 carrots, peeled and sliced
  thinly**
175 g (6 oz) dried red lentils
**4 tomatoes, de-seeded and
  chopped**
2 bay leaves
2 teaspoons dried mixed herbs
**1.2 litres (2 pints) vegetable
  stock**
**salt and freshly ground black
  pepper**

For the croûtons
**2 slices day-old wholemeal
  bread, crusts removed**
**2 garlic cloves, halved
  lengthways**

*A simple soup that is full of flavour and perfect for lunch
with family or friends.*

1 Spray a large, lidded, non stick saucepan with the cooking
spray and fry the onion, celery stick, celery leaves and carrots
for 5 minutes, stirring regularly. Stir in the lentils, tomatoes,
bay leaves and mixed herbs.

2 Pour in the stock, bring up to the boil, reduce the heat and
simmer, half-covered, for 15–20 minutes until the lentils are
tender, skimming off any foam that rises to the surface. Remove
the bay leaves. Using a food processor, or a hand held blender,
whizz until smooth. Season to taste.

3 Meanwhile, rub both sides of each slice of bread with the
garlic. Cut the bread into cubes and spray with the cooking spray.
In a non stick frying pan, fry the bread, turning occasionally and
spraying with more cooking spray if necessary, until golden and
crisp. Serve the croûtons on top of the soup with some freshly
ground black pepper.

Summer vegetable soup

Serves 4

77 calories per serving

Takes 10 minutes to prepare,
20 minutes to cook

Ⓥ

1 litre (1¾ pints) hot vegetable
stock

a bunch of spring onions,
finely chopped

1 garlic clove, crushed

3 celery sticks, finely sliced

1 large courgette, chopped

125 g (4½ oz) fine green
beans, sliced

1 tablespoon pesto

about 12 fresh basil leaves,
torn into shreds

25 g (1 oz) dried tiny pasta
shapes

50 g (1¾ oz) crisp lettuce or
Chinese leaf lettuce, finely
shredded

salt and freshly ground black
pepper

*This delicious soup is one of the nicest ways to eat your
greens.*

1 In a large lidded saucepan, bring the stock to the boil.

2 Add the spring onions, garlic, celery, courgette and green
beans. Return to the boil and then reduce the heat. Cover and
simmer for 10 minutes.

3 Add the pesto, basil and pasta shapes and cook until they
are just tender, about 6–8 minutes. Add the shredded lettuce
or Chinese leaf lettuce and cook for another 2 minutes. Season
to taste.

4 Ladle the soup into warmed bowls and serve immediately.

Tip... Avoid overcooking the soup; the vegetables should
retain their fresh flavours and colours.

Variation... Use well washed spinach leaves instead of
lettuce or Chinese leaf lettuce.

Roasted pepper soup with Parmesan crisps

Serves 4

120 calories per serving

Takes 10 minutes to prepare,
35 minutes to cook

A brightly coloured soup with cheesy little bites.

6 red peppers, de-seeded and sliced

3 whole garlic cloves

2 teaspoons olive oil

2 fresh rosemary sprigs, leaves only

1 litre (1¾ pints) hot vegetable stock

For the crisps

8 teaspoons freshly grated Parmesan cheese

2 teaspoons fresh thyme leaves

freshly ground black pepper

1 Preheat the oven to Gas Mark 6/200°C/fan oven 180°C. Line a roasting tin with foil and add the peppers and whole garlic cloves. Drizzle over the oil and add the rosemary, tossing to coat the vegetables. Roast for 30 minutes until softened and lightly charred. Remove the tin from the oven, leaving the oven on. Pop the garlic from their skins.

2 Place the peppers, garlic and their juices in a large saucepan with about a third of the stock. Using a food processor, or a hand held blender, whizz until roughly smooth. Return to the pan, add the remaining stock and heat through until hot.

3 Meanwhile, mix together the grated Parmesan, thyme and a little black pepper. Place teaspoons of the mixture, well spaced apart, on a non stick baking tray, making eight piles. There is no need to push them down. Bake for 5 minutes until golden. Leave to cool on the tray for a few minutes before carefully transferring to a plate. The cheese spreads as it melts and cooks to look like a crisp with little holes.

4 Serve the soup in warmed bowls with two Parmesan crisps each.

Tips... You can use a variety of coloured peppers in this soup although red, orange and yellow are the best since they are sweeter.

If your baking tray is not non stick, use non stick baking parchment or a Teflon sheet on top.

Courgette and potato soup

Serves 2

123 calories per serving

Takes 15 minutes to prepare,
25 minutes to cook

Ⓥ

❄

calorie controlled cooking
  spray

1 small onion, chopped finely

1 garlic clove, crushed

150 g (5½ oz) potatoes, peeled
  and diced

225 g (8 oz) courgettes, grated
  coarsely

1 teaspoon ground coriander

600 ml (20 fl oz) vegetable
  stock

2 tablespoons light soy sauce

freshly ground black pepper

1 tablespoon chopped fresh
  coriander, to garnish

*The soy sauce adds salt to this recipe so you shouldn't
need to add any. Check the seasoning before serving and
add more soy sauce if necessary.*

1 Spray a large non stick saucepan with the cooking spray.
Place the pan on the heat and add the onion and garlic. Cook
over a medium heat for 5 minutes until the onion has softened,
but not browned. Add the potatoes, courgettes and ground
coriander and cook for a further 2–3 minutes.

2 Add the stock and soy sauce and bring to the boil. Reduce
the heat and simmer for 15 minutes, until the potatoes have
broken down.

3 Season to taste with freshly ground black pepper and ladle
into two warmed soup bowls. Garnish with the fresh coriander
and serve.

Variation... To make a creamier soup, stir in 75 g (2¾ oz) of
low fat soft cheese.

Olive tabbouleh

Serves 2
263 calories per serving
Takes 10 minutes + cooling
Ⓥ

300 ml (10 fl oz) hot vegetable
stock
80 g (3 oz) dried bulgar wheat
2 celery sticks, chopped finely
3 tablespoons mixed
fresh herbs (e.g. parsley,
coriander, oregano, mint)
3 vine tomatoes, de-seeded
and diced
2 spring onions, chopped
60 g (2 oz) stoned black olives
in brine, drained and halved
1 lemon, finely grated zest of
½ and the lemon cut into
wedges to serve

Serve with a warmed mini pitta bread per person.

1 Place the stock in a small lidded saucepan and bring to the boil. Add the bulgar wheat, cover and simmer for 5 minutes. Remove from the heat, stir and leave to cool for 15 minutes – most of the liquid should have been absorbed by then.

2 Stir in the remaining ingredients and serve with the lemon wedges to squeeze over.

Tip... Bulgar wheat is a great store cupboard ingredient. Use it for packed lunches or serve it hot as a main meal accompaniment.

Fiesta bean salad

Serves 1
428 calories per serving
Takes 5 minutes
Ⓥ

½ x 410 g can mixed pulses,
drained and rinsed

½ x 198 g can sweetcorn with
peppers, drained

75 g (2¾ oz) cherry tomatoes,
halved

½ avocado, peeled, stoned and
diced

2 tablespoons fat free French
dressing

1 Little Gem lettuce heart,
leaves separated

This salad is a colourful blend of salad vegetables and storecupboard ingredients.

1 Mix the pulses, sweetcorn with peppers, cherry tomatoes and avocado together with 1 tablespoon of the dressing.

2 Place the lettuce leaves in a bowl, drizzle with the second tablespoon of dressing and pile the pulse mixture on top to serve.

Carrot and sunflower seed salad

Serves 4
206 calories per serving
Takes 10 minutes
Ⓥ

2 tablespoons sunflower
 seeds
1 tablespoon pumpkin seeds
8 large carrots, peeled and
 grated coarsely
2 tablespoons soy sauce
a bunch of fresh coriander,
 chopped
2 teaspoons toasted sesame
 oil
1 tablespoon runny honey
salt and freshly ground black
 pepper

*This fresh crunchy salad has fragrant Japanese style
flavourings.*

1 Mix all the ingredients together in a large bowl. Check the
seasoning and serve.

Mediterranean pasta salad

Serves 4
353 calories per serving
Takes 25 minutes
Ⓥ

240 g (8½ oz) dried penne or other pasta shapes

2 red onions, cut into thin wedges

4 courgettes, cut lengthways into long strips

2 red peppers, de-seeded and sliced

2 aubergines, sliced lengthways into long thin pieces

calorie controlled cooking spray

100 g (3½ oz) Feta cheese

a bunch of fresh mint, chopped

2 garlic cloves, crushed

2 tablespoons balsamic vinegar

salt and freshly ground black pepper

This is an ideal recipe for a griddle pan. Otherwise grill the vegetables in batches under the grill or bake them in a hot oven.

1 Bring a saucepan of water to the boil, add the pasta and cook according to the packet instructions. Drain.

2 Meanwhile, lay the vegetables in one layer on a griddle pan and season. Spray with the cooking spray and grill for 4–5 minutes until they are golden and beginning to crisp. You may have to grill the vegetables in several batches depending on the size of your griddle pan. Place them in a large bowl.

3 Add the cooked pasta, Feta cheese, mint, garlic and balsamic vinegar to the bowl, check the seasoning, toss together and serve.

Warm roasted squash salad

Serves 4

186 calories per serving

Takes 15 minutes to prepare,
45–60 minutes to cook

Ⓥ

700 g (1 lb 9 oz) butternut
squash, peeled, de-seeded
and cut into wedges

a generous pinch of dried
chilli flakes

1 teaspoon coriander seeds,
crushed lightly

2 tablespoons balsamic
vinegar

calorie controlled cooking
spray

85 g bag wild rocket

410 g can chick peas, drained
and rinsed

1 red onion, sliced

½ pomegranate, seeds
removed and reserved

60 g (2 oz) low fat soft cheese
with garlic and herbs

2 tablespoons skimmed milk

juice of ½ a lemon

*This autumnal salad makes the most of the sweet
butternut squash flesh, but you can use other varieties
such as pumpkin.*

1 Preheat the oven to Gas Mark 6/200°C/fan oven 180°C.
Put the squash in a bowl and toss together with the chilli
flakes, coriander seeds and balsamic vinegar. Tip on to a non
stick baking tray and spray with the cooking spray. Roast in
the oven for 45–60 minutes until roasted and tender.

2 Meanwhile, divide the rocket, chick peas, onion and
pomegranate seeds between four plates.

3 In a bowl, mix together the soft cheese, skimmed milk and
lemon juice. Divide the roasted squash between the salad
plates and drizzle with the dressing.

Feta stack salad

Serves 1
314 calories per serving
Takes 5 minutes
Ⓥ

This scrummy lunch is sweet, salty, crunchy and soft, making it totally mouthwatering.

1 In a shallow bowl, mix together the orange juice, oil and ginger. Season generously with freshly ground black pepper, add the sliced Feta and toss to coat.

2 Put the salad leaves on a plate and scatter over the celery and carrot. Top with a few slices of beetroot and then the Feta and repeat the layers until both are used up. Drizzle over any remaining dressing, sprinkle with the linseeds and serve immediately.

juice of ½ an orange
2 teaspoons toasted walnut oil
15 g (½ oz) stem ginger in syrup, drained and chopped finely
60 g (2 oz) reduced fat Feta cheese, cut into thin slices
¼ x 150 g bag herb salad leaves
1 celery stick, sliced finely
1 small carrot, peeled and grated
50 g (1¾ oz) crinkle cut pickled beetroot slices, drained
1 teaspoon golden linseeds
freshly ground black pepper

Light bites

Pizza style bruschetta

Serves 4
214 calories per serving
Takes 15 minutes
🟡

225 g (8 oz) ciabatta

1 garlic clove, halved

3 ripe tomatoes, chopped roughly

400 g can artichoke hearts in water, drained and quartered

75 g (2¾ oz) light mozzarella cheese, drained and diced

1 tablespoon fresh thyme leaves

salt and freshly ground black pepper

Serve with a mixed leaf salad, tossed with fat free vinaigrette dressing.

1 Preheat the grill to a medium setting. Slice the ciabatta in half horizontally and then cut each section into two pieces. Toast lightly on both sides under the grill and then rub the garlic on to the cut sides of the toasted bread.

2 In a bowl, mix the chopped tomatoes with seasoning and then press these on to the ciabatta. Top with the pieces of artichoke heart, mozzarella and thyme. Season lightly with freshly ground black pepper and grill for 4–5 minutes until the cheese is bubbling and golden.

Mushroom and herb soufflé omelette

Serves 1
208 calories per serving
Takes 15 minutes
Ⓥ

**calorie controlled cooking
spray**
**50 g (1¾ oz) mushrooms,
sliced**
2 spring onions, sliced
1 garlic clove, sliced
2 eggs, separated
**3 tablespoons chopped fresh
mixed herbs, e.g. parsley,
chives, basil**

*Soufflé omelettes are not difficult to make and more filling
than normal ones.*

1 Lightly spray a small non stick frying pan with the cooking
spray and heat until hot. Add the mushrooms, spring onions
and garlic and stir fry for 5 minutes until the mushrooms begin
to brown.

2 Beat together the egg yolks.

3 In a clean, grease-free bowl, whisk the egg whites until they
form soft peaks. Carefully fold the egg yolks into the whites
together with the herbs.

4 Add the egg mixture to the pan, spreading it out evenly. Cook
for 2–3 minutes until golden on the bottom. Fold in half and
slide out of the pan to serve immediately.

Variation... Try adding 25 g (1 oz) of crumbled Stilton cheese
to the pan on top of the egg mixture.

Cheesy mustard puddings

Serves 4

143 calories per serving

Takes 10 minutes to prepare
+ 5 minutes standing,
15 minutes to cook

Ⓥ

75 g (2¾ oz) fresh white
  breadcrumbs

2 eggs, beaten

2 teaspoons wholegrain
  mustard

200 ml (7 fl oz) skimmed milk

75 g (2¾ oz) half fat Red
  Leicester cheese, grated

salt and freshly ground black
  pepper

Made in individual ramekin dishes, these cheesy little pots make an excellent starter or light snack. Serve them hot with a crisp green salad tossed with a little vinaigrette.

1 Preheat the oven to Gas Mark 5/190°C/fan oven 170°C.

2 Mix together the breadcrumbs, eggs, mustard, milk, cheese and seasoning. Divide the mixture between four ramekin dishes. Leave to stand for 5 minutes.

3 Bake the dishes in the oven for 15 minutes. The puddings will rise slightly like a soufflé, so you need to serve them at once.

Tip... Try and use crumbs made from bread that is a couple of days old; they soak up the moisture better.

Variation... The Red Leicester cheese gives these puddings a rich colour, but use Cheddar cheese if you prefer its flavour.

Rice and vegetable pot

Serves 4

287 calories per serving

Takes 25 minutes to prepare,
45 minutes to cook

Ⓥ
❄

225 g (8 oz) dried brown rice

225 g (8 oz) carrots, peeled
and diced

1 onion, chopped

1 green pepper, de-seeded and
diced

1 red pepper, de-seeded and
diced

150 g (5½ oz) mushrooms,
sliced

2 tablespoons dark soy sauce

700 ml (1¼ pints) vegetable
stock

2 tablespoons tomato purée

100 g (3½ oz) frozen peas

*This tasty mixture of brown rice and vegetables is
delicious for a filling lunchtime snack.*

1 Place the rice in a large lidded saucepan with the carrots,
onion, peppers and mushrooms. Mix together the soy sauce,
stock and tomato purée and then add this mixture to the rice
and vegetables.

2 Bring everything to the boil. Reduce the heat, cover and
simmer gently for 35 minutes, stirring from time to time.

3 Stir in the frozen peas. Cover and cook for a further
5–10 minutes, until all the liquid has been absorbed and
the rice is tender. Serve warm, or chill in the fridge and
serve as a rice salad.

Variation... Try adding a tablespoon of curry powder to the
rice while it is cooking, to add a hint of spice.

Avocado wrap

Serves 1

289 calories per serving

Takes 10 minutes + chilling (optional)

Ⓥ

4 **Little Gem lettuce leaves, shredded**

¼ **avocado, cut into small chunks**

1 **tablespoon Weight Watchers Extra Light Mayonnaise**

1 **tablespoon low fat natural yogurt**

1 **soft tortilla wrap**

½ **tablespoon cress**

a selection of salad vegetables

A simple quick wrap that tastes simply wonderful.

1 Put the shredded lettuce and avocado into a small bowl. In a ramekin, mix the mayonnaise with the yogurt. Pour the mayonnaise mixture over the lettuce mixture and carefully combine.

2 Lay some cling film on a flat surface and place the tortilla wrap on it. Spoon the lettuce mixture in a strip along the centre of the wrap. Sprinkle it with the cress and then fold the two sides over the filling to form a tube. Hold it firmly together until you can wrap the cling film round the tortilla and seal well. If you have time, chill in the fridge for at least an hour.

3 Remove the cling film and make a diagonal cut across the centre of the wrap. Serve the two halves with the salad vegetables.

Pesto and roasted pepper bagel

Serves 1
304 calories per serving
Takes 12 minutes

 Ⓥ

½ red pepper, de-seeded
80 g (3 oz) bagel, halved
1 teaspoon pesto
25 g (1 oz) low fat soft cheese
15 g (½ oz) watercress

Roasted or grilled peppers have a lovely sweet flavour and soften in the cooking process, which also makes them easier to digest.

1 Preheat the grill to its highest setting. Press the pepper half flat with your hand and place on the grill rack, skin side up, close to the heat.

2 Grill for about 5 minutes until the skin blackens and blisters. Remove from the heat, place in a plastic bag and leave for a few minutes until cool enough to handle. Peel off the skin and then cut the pepper into strips.

3 Toast the bagel halves lightly. Mix the pesto into the soft cheese and spread on the bottom half of the bagel. Add the red pepper strips and watercress to the bottom half of the bagel, cover with the top half and serve.

Tip... If you don't have time to grill the pepper, you can buy jars of ready roasted and peeled peppers in brine. These can also be added to salads, pasta sauces and stir fries.

Piperade

Serves 2
243 calories per serving
Takes 30 minutes
🟡

1 red pepper, halved and
   de-seeded
1 green pepper, halved and
   de-seeded
calorie controlled cooking
   spray
1 onion, chopped finely
1 garlic clove, crushed
4 ripe tomatoes
4 eggs, beaten lightly
cayenne pepper or chilli
   powder, to taste
salt and freshly ground black
   pepper

A classic Basque dish with peppers, tomatoes and eggs.

1 Preheat the grill to high and grill the pepper halves, skin side up, until charred. Pop them into a plastic bag and leave until cool enough to handle.

2 Meanwhile, heat a non stick frying pan, spray with the cooking spray and fry the onion and garlic until soft, adding a splash of water if they start to stick. Peel and dice the peppers.

3 Add the tomatoes and peppers to the pan and cook until you have a thick pureé. Lower the heat and stir in the eggs.

4 Add the cayenne pepper or chilli powder, season and continue stirring until the eggs have cooked to a cream. Serve immediately.

Garlic bread with pickled vegetable salsa

Serves 2

276 calories per serving

Takes 10 minutes to prepare,
  15 minutes to cook

Ⓥ

**½ granary baguette, halved
  lengthways and then
  crossways to make four
  pieces**

**100 g (3½ oz) low fat garlic
  roulé cheese**

For the pickled vegetable salsa

**2 carrots, peeled and chopped
  finely**

**1 small red onion, chopped
  finely**

**2 tablespoons capers, drained
  and rinsed**

**2 pickled gherkins, chopped
  finely**

1 garlic clove, crushed

**2 tablespoons white wine
  vinegar**

2 teaspoons caster sugar

1 teaspoon olive oil

**salt and freshly ground black
  pepper**

*This recipe is great as a light meal and wonderful served
with baked fish.*

1 Preheat the oven to Gas Mark 4/180°C/fan oven 160°C.
Spread the bread with the roulé and then reassemble as a loaf
and wrap in foil. Bake for 15 minutes until hot.

2 Meanwhile, make the pickle by mixing together all the
ingredients in a bowl. Serve the garlic bread with the pickle
on the side.

Tip... The pickled vegetable salsa is good made a few hours
in advance and left to marinate.

Variation... You could substitute 25 g (1 oz) of sun-dried
tomatoes, soaked in boiling water and then drained and
chopped, for the capers or gherkins, and/or add some
stoned olives.

Fiery squash cakes

Serves 2
164 calories per serving
Takes 30 minutes
Ⓥ

200 g (7 oz) butternut squash, peeled, de-seeded and diced
200 g (7 oz) potatoes, peeled and diced
1 egg
¼ teaspoon ground coriander
¼ teaspoon ground allspice
1 tablespoon chopped fresh coriander
2 spring onions, sliced finely
calorie controlled cooking spray
salt and freshly ground black pepper

For the chilli sauce

a generous pinch of dried chilli flakes
1 tablespoon white wine vinegar
1 teaspoon artificial sweetener
2 teaspoons tomato purée

Serve with a generous watercress and tomato salad.

1 Bring a large lidded saucepan of water to the boil, add the squash and potatoes, bring back to the boil, cover and simmer for 15 minutes until tender.

2 Meanwhile, bring a small saucepan of water to the boil, add the egg and simmer for 10 minutes. Drain and plunge the egg into cold water.

3 Drain the squash and potatoes, rinse in cold water until cold and drain again. Return to the saucepan and mash with a potato masher until smooth. Peel the egg and chop roughly. Add the egg to the potatoes and squash along with the ground coriander, allspice, fresh coriander, spring onions and seasoning. Shape into four small cakes.

4 Heat a non stick frying pan until hot and spray with the cooking spray. Gently fry the cakes for 5 minutes, turning until golden.

5 Meanwhile, mix together the chilli flakes, vinegar, sweetener, tomato purée and 2 tablespoons of cold water in a bowl. Serve two cakes each with the chilli sauce.

Spiced lentil dip with crudités

Serves 1

479 calories per serving

Takes 5 minutes to prepare + cooling, 30 minutes to cook

Ⓥ

50 g (1¾ oz) dried red lentils
300 ml (10 fl oz) vegetable stock
½ teaspoon ground cumin
1 teaspoon curry powder
2 teaspoons sesame seeds

To serve

celery sticks
red pepper slices
carrot sticks
2 wholewheat Krisprolls

This makes a delicious healthier alternative to houmous.

1 Place the lentils and stock in a small lidded saucepan. Bring to the boil, continue boiling for 10 minutes and then cover and cook for a further 20 minutes until the lentils are mushy. Keep an eye on the pan, as you may need to add extra water to the lentils if they get too dry. You should be able to mash the cooked mixture easily with a fork to form a rough slightly wet purée – it will thicken on cooling.

2 Dry fry the spices and sesame seeds for 1–2 minutes until their aroma is released, add to the lentil purée and stir well. Leave to cool before chilling.

3 Serve the dip with the vegetable sticks and slices as well as the Krisprolls.

Tip... This is great for a party or lunch box – you could also use strips of pitta bread (60 g/2 oz per person), in place of the Krisprolls.

Grilled aubergine sandwich

Serves 2

306 calories per serving

Takes 15 minutes to prepare,
15 minutes to cook

Ⓥ

1 aubergine

1 tablespoon olive oil

225 g can chopped tomatoes
with herbs

2 tablespoons sun-dried
tomato purée

1 red pepper, de-seeded and
diced

100 g (3½ oz) light mozzarella
cheese, drained and diced

1 tablespoon dried
breadcrumbs

salt and freshly ground black
pepper

*Fast, but full of flavour, this is perfect for a quick lunch
for two.*

1 Preheat the grill to medium-high. Thinly slice the aubergine
horizontally. Season each slice and brush lightly with the olive
oil. Grill for 10 minutes, turning halfway through.

2 In a small pan, mix together the chopped tomatoes, tomato
purée and red pepper. Heat through. Sandwich two aubergine
slices together with some of the tomato mixture. Sprinkle the
tops with some of the mozzarella and breadcrumbs. Repeat
with the remaining slices and ingredients and return to the grill
for 5 minutes, until the cheese melts and begins to brown.

Welsh rarebit with roasted tomatoes

Serves 1

245 calories per serving

Takes 10 minutes to prepare,
20 minutes to cook

Ⓥ

3 plum tomatoes, halved

1 teaspoon balsamic vinegar

1 thick slice bread

1 teaspoon low fat spread

25 g (1 oz) half fat Cheddar
cheese, grated

1 teaspoon plain flour

½ teaspoon English mustard

4 tablespoons beer

salt and freshly ground black
pepper

Cheesy toast is delicious served with oven roasted tomatoes.

1 Preheat the oven to Gas Mark 6/200°C/fan oven 180°C. Place the tomatoes on a non stick baking tray. Season well and drizzle each half with a little of the vinegar. Roast for 20 minutes.

2 Meanwhile, toast the bread until golden and spread with the low fat spread.

3 Place the cheese, flour, mustard and beer in a small pan and heat gently, stirring constantly until the cheese has melted. Spoon over the toast and grill for 2–3 minutes, until bubbling and lightly browned. Serve with the roasted tomatoes.

Lunchbox pea and mint frittatas

Serves 4

140 calories per serving

Takes 8 minutes to prepare + cooling, 12 minutes to cook

Ⓥ

calorie controlled cooking spray

200 g (7 oz) frozen peas

3 eggs, plus 2 egg whites

2 tablespoons half fat crème fraîche

2 tablespoons skimmed milk

2 tablespoons chopped fresh mint

15 g (½ oz) freshly grated Parmesan cheese

salt and freshly ground black pepper

These are best when served at room temperature, rather than piping hot or fridge cold. Serve with a mixture of tender salad leaves.

1 Preheat the oven to Gas Mark 4/180°C/fan oven 160°C. Lightly spray eight holes of a non stick muffin tin with the cooking spray.

2 Bring a saucepan of water to the boil. Add the peas, bring back to the boil and then drain the peas immediately. Divide between the greased muffin tin holes.

3 In a bowl, beat the eggs and egg whites with the crème fraîche and milk. Season and then stir in the mint and Parmesan cheese. Pour on top of the peas.

4 Bake the frittatas in the oven for 12 minutes until firm, puffy and lightly golden.

5 Remove from the tin and leave to cool slightly before serving each person with two frittatas.

Speedy suppers

Red hot pepper pasta

Serves 4
343 calories per serving
Takes 30 minutes
Ⓥ

250 g (9 oz) dried spinach, tomato or plain pasta shapes

200 g (7 oz) watercress, chopped coarsely

100 g (3½ oz) Feta cheese, crumbled

1 tablespoon toasted pine nut kernels

salt and freshly ground black pepper

For the sauce

4 red peppers, halved and de-seeded

2 garlic cloves, crushed

2 tablespoons balsamic vinegar

1–2 small red chillies, de-seeded and chopped finely

This pasta dish with a kick is great as an after work supper or for lunch with friends.

1 Bring a large saucepan of water to the boil, add the pasta and cook according to the packet instructions, until al dente. Preheat the grill to a high heat.

2 Meanwhile, to make the sauce, grill the red peppers skin side up until blistered and blackened. Place in a plastic bag and leave until cool enough to handle.

3 Peel off the charred skin from the peppers and discard. Using a food processor, or a hand held blender, whizz the pepper flesh with the other sauce ingredients, adding a few tablespoons of water, or enough to make a smooth purée.

4 Drain the pasta and return to the pan. Add the sauce and remaining ingredients. Toss and then serve immediately.

Sweet and sour tofu and vegetables

Serves 4
360 calories per serving
Takes 20 minutes
Ⓥ

240 g (8½ oz) dried brown rice
calorie controlled cooking
    spray
1 onion, sliced
1 courgette, sliced thinly
1 carrot, peeled and cut into
    sticks
1 red pepper, de-seeded and
    sliced
250 g (9 oz) tofu, cubed
75 g (2¾ oz) frozen peas
227 g can pineapple cubes in
    natural juice
3 tablespoons tomato purée
2 tablespoons white wine
    vinegar
2 teaspoons artificial
    sweetener

The tang of sweet and sour gives tofu a new lease of life in this quick stir fry.

1 Bring a large lidded saucepan of water to the boil, add the rice, cover and cook according to the packet instructions. Drain well and keep hot.

2 Meanwhile, lightly spray a large non stick frying pan with the cooking spray and heat until hot. Add the onion, courgette, carrot and pepper and stir fry for 3–4 minutes until just tender.

3 Add the tofu, peas, pineapple and juice, tomato purée, vinegar and sweetener. Cook, stirring, for 1–2 minutes until everything is hot. Serve with the brown rice.

Variation... If you prefer, you can use 250 g (9 oz) of dried noodles instead of the rice.

Red wine mushrooms with polenta mash

Serves 2
392 calories per serving
Takes 15 minutes
Ⓥ

600 ml (20 fl oz) vegetable
  stock
1 teaspoon cornflour
calorie controlled cooking
  spray
3 shallots, sliced finely
1 garlic clove, crushed
250 g (9 oz) chestnut and
  oyster mushrooms, sliced
  thickly
125 ml (4 fl oz) red wine
2 tablespoons cranberry sauce
1 tablespoon fresh thyme
  leaves
100 g (3½ oz) dried quick cook
  polenta
1–2 teaspoons Dijon mustard,
  to taste
30 g (1¼ oz) Parmesan
  cheese, grated
salt and freshly ground black
  pepper

Mushrooms are a great alternative to meat due to their dense texture and flavoursome punch. Serve with cooked broccoli, green beans and 1 tablespoon of peas per person.

1 Pour 400 ml (14 fl oz) of the vegetable stock into a large pan and bring to the boil. Dissolve the cornflour in the remaining stock.

2 Meanwhile, heat a deep non stick frying pan and spray with the cooking spray. Add the shallots, garlic and mushrooms and cook for 5 minutes until just starting to brown.

3 Add the red wine to the mushrooms and bubble for a minute until almost evaporated. Stir in the cornflour mixture, cranberry sauce and thyme. Gently heat for 1–2 minutes until thickened. Check the seasoning and keep warm.

4 Once the pan of stock is boiling, add the polenta and cook for 1–2 minutes, stirring until thickened. Be careful, as it will bubble like a volcano. Stir in the mustard and Parmesan. Season and serve immediately with the mushrooms and red wine sauce.

Vegetable spring rolls with sweet chilli sauce

Serves 4
257 calories per serving
Takes 30 minutes

A pack of ready prepared stir fry vegetables makes light work for these crispy little spring rolls. If you prefer, use the same weight of mixed vegetables, such as carrots, peppers, onions, bean sprouts and Chinese leaf lettuce, cut into thin shreds.

calorie controlled cooking spray
300 g (10½ oz) stir fry vegetables
1 teaspoon grated fresh root ginger
2 garlic cloves, crushed
¼ teaspoon Chinese five spice
1 tablespoon soy sauce
110 g (4 oz) water chestnuts, drained and sliced
4 x 45 g (1½ oz) filo pastry sheets, measuring 50 x 24 cm (20 x 9½ inches)
2 teaspoons sunflower oil
1 teaspoon sesame oil

For the sauce
1 tablespoon soy sauce
3 tablespoons sweet chilli sauce
juice of ½ a lime

1 Heat a wok or large non stick frying pan and spray with the cooking spray. Add the vegetables, ginger, garlic and Chinese five spice and stir fry for 2 minutes. Add the soy sauce and water chestnuts and remove the pan from the heat. Leave to cool slightly.

2 Preheat the oven to Gas Mark 6/200°C/fan oven 180°C.

3 Cut each sheet of filo pastry in half widthways. Stack the pieces of pastry together and keep them covered with a clean damp tea towel while you work.

4 Mix the sunflower oil and sesame oil together in a small bowl. Take a piece of filo and brush lightly with the blended oil. Fold it in half to create a long narrow rectangle and place a spoonful of vegetables at one end. Roll up the pastry, folding in the sides to hold in the filling. Place on a non stick baking tray. Repeat with the rest of the filo sheets and filling to make eight spring rolls and then brush the rolls with any remaining oil.

5 Bake for 13–15 minutes until crisp and golden. Mix the sauce ingredients together and serve with the spring rolls.

Quick peanut noodles

Serves 4
454 calories per serving
Takes 25 minutes
Ⓥ

300 g (10½ oz) dried medium egg noodles
calorie controlled cooking spray
2 carrots, peeled and shredded
½ cucumber, shredded
a bunch of spring onions, cut into 2.5 cm (1 inch) lengths and shredded
a small bunch of fresh coriander, chopped

For the sauce
2 tablespoons crunchy peanut butter
juice of 2 limes
2 tablespoons soy sauce
1 teaspoon dried chilli flakes

In this recipe, noodles are tossed with raw shredded vegetables and served with a light lime, peanut and soy sauce for a fresh tasting and quick lunch or supper.

1 Bring a saucepan of water to the boil, add the noodles and cook according to the packet instructions. Drain thoroughly.

2 Meanwhile, make the sauce. Put all the ingredients in a small saucepan and heat gently, stirring, until the peanut butter melts. Stir in 4 tablespoons of water to give a fairly thin consistency.

3 Heat a wok or large non stick frying pan and spray with the cooking spray. Add the noodles and vegetables, toss together and then pour the sauce over and sprinkle in the fresh coriander. Toss together again and serve.

Broad bean and leek tortilla

Serves 4
208 calories per serving
Takes 35 minutes
Ⓥ

250 g (9 oz) fresh broad beans
   or frozen broad beans,
   defrosted
2 leeks, sliced
2 courgettes, sliced thinly
1 tablespoon chopped fresh
   mint
6 eggs, beaten
75 g (2¾ oz) light mozzarella
   cheese, drained and cut into
   tiny cubes
salt and freshly ground black
   pepper

A selection of early summer vegetables makes this quick meal perfect for those longer evenings.

1 Bring a saucepan of water to the boil, add the broad beans and cook for 5 minutes, adding the leeks and courgettes for the last minute. Drain and refresh under cold running water. Slip the skins from the broad beans to reveal the bright green bean beneath.

2 Heat a large non stick frying pan with a heatproof handle and dry fry the vegetables with the mint for 2–3 minutes to remove any surplus water. Season the eggs and then pour into the pan over the vegetables. Cook gently for 6 minutes, or until almost set.

3 Preheat the grill to a medium heat. Sprinkle the mozzarella over the top of the tortilla and brown under the grill for 2–3 minutes until bubbling.

4 Cool slightly before slicing into four and serving straight from the pan.

Vegetarian goulash

Serves 4
112 calories per serving
Takes 20 minutes
Ⓥ

calorie controlled cooking
   spray
1 onion, chopped roughly
1 garlic clove, crushed
2 red or green peppers,
   de-seeded and cut into
   eighths
3 portabello mushrooms,
   quartered
400 g can artichoke hearts in
   water, drained and quartered
1 tablespoon rose harissa
1 tablespoon paprika
1 tablespoon sun-dried tomato
   paste
400 g can chopped tomatoes
300 ml (10 fl oz) vegetable
   stock
1 tablespoon finely chopped
   fresh flat leaf parsley, to
   garnish

The key to this dish is to make sure all the vegetables are
cut to the same size.

1 Heat a large non stick saucepan and spray with the cooking
spray. Add the onion and cook for 3–4 minutes until softened
but not coloured. Add the garlic, peppers, mushrooms and
artichokes and cook for 3 minutes until starting to brown.

2 Stir in the harissa, paprika and tomato paste and cook for
1 minute. Add the tomatoes and vegetable stock, bring to
the boil and simmer for 10 minutes until thickened. Serve
immediately in shallow bowls, scattered with the parsley.

Creamy bulgar mushrooms

Serves 2
312 calories per serving
Takes 30 minutes
Ⓥ

calorie controlled cooking spray
4 large field mushrooms, sliced
1 onion, cut into wedges
2 garlic cloves, sliced
110 g (4 oz) dried bulgar wheat
600 ml (20 fl oz) vegetable stock
50 g (1¾ oz) broccoli florets
1 tablespoon mushroom ketchup (optional)
2 tablespoons chopped fresh parsley
3 tablespoons low fat soft cheese
salt and freshly ground black pepper

Bulgar wheat has a lovely nutty flavour.

1 Lightly spray a lidded non stick frying pan with the cooking spray and heat until hot. Add the mushrooms and onion and stir fry for 5 minutes. Add the garlic and cook for a further 2 minutes.

2 Add the bulgar wheat and stock and bring to the boil. Cover with a tight fitting lid and cook for 5 minutes. Add the broccoli and cook for a further 5 minutes until the bulgar wheat is cooked, the stock has been absorbed and the broccoli is tender.

3 Stir in the mushroom ketchup, if using, parsley and soft cheese and season.

Variation... Dried mushrooms work well in this recipe. Use 25 g (1 oz) of dried porcini or mixed mushrooms in place of the fresh, soaking them according to the packet instructions and using the soaking water in place of some of the stock.

Grilled vegetable kebabs with a hot tomato glaze

Serves 4

88 calories per serving

Takes 5 minutes to prepare,
 20 minutes to cook

Ⓥ

1 aubergine, sliced into
 2.5 cm (1 inch) thick rounds
 and then quartered

1 red or yellow pepper,
 de-seeded and cut into
 chunks

2 courgettes, sliced thickly

4 teaspoons olive oil

2 tomatoes, skinned,
 de-seeded and chopped
 finely

1 shallot, chopped finely

4 teaspoons horseradish
 sauce

salt and freshly ground black
 pepper

The heat in the tomato glaze turns these vegetable kebabs into something a little bit special.

1 Preheat the grill to medium-high. Remove the rack and line the grill tray with foil.

2 Thread the aubergine, pepper and courgettes on to 4 small skewers. Brush with the oil and season. Grill for 15–20 minutes, turning and brushing with oil frequently, until the vegetables have softened and coloured.

3 Meanwhile, make the glaze by mixing together the tomatoes, shallot and horseradish sauce in a small bowl. Stir in any remaining oil and then use to brush over the vegetables for the last 5 minutes of grilling.

4 To serve, brush the kebabs with the remaining glaze and season to taste.

Tip... If using wooden skewers, soak them in water for 30 minutes beforehand to prevent them from burning.

Giant shells with spinach and basil pesto

Serves 2
406 calories per serving
Takes 25 minutes
Ⓥ

**150 g (5½ oz) dried giant
pasta shells**
**calorie controlled cooking
spray**
4 spring onions, chopped
75 g (2¾ oz) spinach, washed

For the pesto
15 g (½ oz) Parmesan cheese
15 g (½ oz) pine nut kernels
25 g packet fresh basil leaves
1 small garlic clove, peeled
**2 teaspoons extra virgin olive
oil**

*When you make your own pesto, not only do you get
a wonderful fresh basil flavour but you can make it
healthier too.*

1 For the pesto, using a food processor, or a hand held blender,
whizz the Parmesan and pine nut kernels to crumbs. Add the
basil, reserving a few leaves for garnish, and the garlic and
whizz again. Add the oil and blend to a thick paste. Set aside.

2 Bring a large saucepan of water to the boil, add the pasta
and cook according to the packet instructions. Drain well,
reserving 4 tablespoons of the cooking liquid. Return the pasta
to the pan.

3 Meanwhile, spray a non stick frying pan with the cooking
spray and heat until hot. Add the spring onions and stir fry
for 2 minutes until softened. Add the spinach and cook for
a further minute until just wilted. Remove from the heat.

4 Stir the spinach mixture into the pasta with the pesto
and reserved cooking liquid. Gently warm through, stirring
continuously until hot. Serve garnished with the reserved
basil leaves.

Tip... The pesto will keep in the fridge, covered, for 5 days.

Cauliflower Provençale

Serves 4

116 calories per serving

Takes 20 minutes to prepare,
10 minutes to cook

Ⓥ

calorie controlled cooking spray

2 courgettes, quartered lengthways

3 garlic cloves, crushed

1½ teaspoons dried mixed herbs

400 g can chopped tomatoes

100 ml (3½ fl oz) boiling water

1 cauliflower, broken into large florets

60 g (2 oz) fresh breadcrumbs

60 g (2 oz) half fat Cheddar cheese, grated

salt and freshly ground black pepper

Serve with a 225 g (8 oz) potato, baked in its skin, per person.

1 Preheat the oven to Gas Mark 7/220°C/fan oven 200°C.

2 Heat a lidded saucepan and spray with the cooking spray. Slice the courgette quarters into chunky pieces and fry for 3 minutes until coloured. Add 2 of the crushed garlic cloves and 1 teaspoon of the dried herbs and cook for a further minute.

3 Stir in the tomatoes and pour in the boiling water. Season and then mix in the cauliflower. Cover the pan and simmer for 10 minutes until the cauliflower is tender.

4 In a bowl, mix the breadcrumbs and cheese together with the remaining garlic and mixed herbs.

5 Transfer the cauliflower and sauce to an ovenproof dish and scatter the breadcrumb mixture all over. Mist with the cooking spray and bake for 10 minutes until crisp and golden. Serve immediately.

Spicy bean quesadillas

Serves 4
421 calories per serving
Takes 25 minutes
Ⓥ

8 x 20 cm (8 inch) flour
   tortillas
420 g can mixed beans in
   chilli sauce
100 g (3½ oz) half fat Cheddar
   cheese, grated
½ red onion, sliced thinly
150 g (5½ oz) mushrooms,
   sliced
1 red or yellow pepper,
   de-seeded and diced
1 red chilli, de-seeded and
   sliced
2 tablespoons chopped fresh
   coriander

*A quesadilla is a Mexican version of a toasted sandwich,
using soft flour tortillas instead of bread. Packed with spicy
beans and Cheddar cheese, these vegetarian quesadillas
are a quick and very nutritious meal, delicious served with
a mixed salad.*

1 Place a large non stick frying pan on the hob to preheat.

2 Meanwhile, lay a tortilla flat on a chopping board, spread a
quarter of the beans over the tortilla and sprinkle with a quarter
of the cheese, onion, mushrooms, pepper, chilli and coriander.
Top with a second tortilla.

3 Transfer to the pan, cook over a medium heat for 2 minutes
and then carefully flip the quesadilla over with the help of a fish
slice and cook for another 1 minute.

4 Repeat with the remaining tortillas and filling ingredients.
Serve the quesadillas cut into wedges.

Variation... Top the cooked quesadillas with 1 tablespoon
of very low fat plain fromage frais.

Mexican stir fry

Serves 4
377 calories per serving
Takes 30 minutes
Ⓥ

1 tablespoon sunflower oil
1 red onion, quartered and sliced
2 garlic cloves, crushed
1 red pepper, de-seeded and chopped
1 yellow pepper, de-seeded and chopped
1 green pepper, de-seeded and chopped
1 teaspoon cayenne pepper
2 teaspoons cumin seeds
2 courgettes, chopped
3 tomatoes, chopped roughly
150 g (5½ oz) baby corn, halved
2 tablespoons fresh coriander, chopped
salt and freshly ground black pepper

To serve
8 medium soft flour tortillas
150 g (5½ oz) 0% fat Greek yogurt

This dish is great to share with friends and it's so simple to make.

1 Heat the oil in a wok or large non stick frying pan, add the onion, garlic and peppers and stir fry for 3–4 minutes. Add the cayenne pepper and cumin seeds and cook for another 2 minutes. Preheat the oven to Gas Mark 5/190°C/fan oven 170°C.

2 Add the courgettes, tomatoes and baby corn and cook for a further 5–7 minutes. Stir in the coriander and season. Spoon into a large serving dish and keep warm.

3 Wrap the tortillas in foil and heat in the preheated oven for 3–4 minutes.

4 To serve, spoon some of the stir fry mixture on to a warmed tortilla and top with a spoonful of Greek yogurt. Roll up the tortilla and eat with your fingers. Allow two tortillas per person.

Pasta in a paper bag

Serves 4
313 calories per serving
Takes 30 minutes
Ⓥ

calorie controlled cooking
  spray
2 small aubergines, diced
2 garlic cloves, sliced
450 g (1 lb) tomatoes, chopped
2 teaspoons dried thyme
320 g jar whole peppers in
  brine, drained and sliced
250 ml (9 fl oz) hot vegetable
  stock
250 g (9 oz) fresh penne
salt and freshly ground black
  pepper

An unusual way of cooking and serving pasta that will get everyone talking.

1 Preheat the oven to Gas Mark 6/200°C/fan oven 180°C. Spray a lidded non stick frying pan with the cooking spray and heat until sizzling. Add the aubergines and stir fry for 2–3 minutes.

2 Add the garlic and continue cooking for 1–2 minutes until golden. Add the tomatoes, thyme, peppers and hot stock. Bring to the boil, cover and simmer for 5 minutes until pulpy. Season.

3 The easiest way to fill the parcels is to place a 40 cm (16 inch) square piece of baking parchment in a bowl. Place a quarter of the pasta in the centre, top with a quarter of the sauce, scrunch the top together and place on a baking tray. Repeat with four other squares of baking parchment and the remaining ingredients.

4 Bake for 12–15 minutes in the oven or until the pasta is just cooked – you will have to open one of the parcels to check. Serve each parcel on a plate and let your guests open their own.

Family favourites

Vegetarian shepherd's pie

Serves 4

343 calories per serving

Takes 40 minutes to prepare,
45 minutes to cook

Y

❄

500 g (1 lb 2 oz) sweet potato,
peeled and cut into even
chunks

calorie controlled cooking
spray

1 onion, chopped finely

2 garlic cloves, crushed

1 celery stick, diced finely

1 carrot, peeled and diced
finely

1 tablespoon chopped fresh
rosemary leaves

125 ml (4 fl oz) red wine

350 g packet Quorn mince

1 tablespoon plain flour

700 g jar passata

220 g can butter beans,
drained and rinsed

25 g (1 oz) half fat Cheddar
cheese, grated

salt and freshly ground black
pepper

An exciting meatless shepherd's pie for all the family.

1 Bring a large lidded saucepan of water to the boil, add the
sweet potato, cover and simmer for 20 minutes. Drain, mash
and season.

2 Meanwhile, preheat the oven to Gas Mark 5/190°C/fan oven
170°C. Heat a non stick saucepan and spray with the cooking
spray. Gently fry the onion, garlic, celery, carrot and rosemary
for 5–8 minutes until beginning to soften. Add the red wine and
bubble for 2 minutes to reduce.

3 Stir in the Quorn mince and flour. Pour in the passata and
cook for 5 minutes. Stir through the butter beans, check the
seasoning and transfer to a 1 litre (1¾ pint) ovenproof dish.

4 Top the Quorn mince with the mash, spreading evenly with
a fork. Sprinkle over the cheese and bake in the oven for
40–45 minutes until golden and bubbling.

Nachos with salsa and guacamole

Serves 4
255 calories per serving
Takes 25 minutes
Ⓥ

450 g (1 lb) ripe tomatoes
a kettleful of boiling water
1 avocado, peeled and stoned
100 g (3½ oz) Quark
1 red onion, finely chopped
juice of a lime
a few drops Tabasco sauce
2 tablespoons chopped fresh
  coriander
salt and freshly ground black
  pepper

For the tortillas
4 x 20 cm (8 inch) flour
  tortillas
calorie controlled cooking
  spray
1 teaspoon smoked paprika

Served with tomato salsa and home baked tortilla chips, this is a great snack for an evening in front of the television.

1 Preheat the oven to Gas Mark 4/180°C/fan oven 160°C. Spray the tortillas with the cooking spray and sprinkle lightly with the smoked paprika. Using kitchen scissors, cut each tortilla into four strips and then into small triangles. Spread out on a baking tray and bake for 6–7 minutes until golden. Leave to cool and crisp up.

2 To make the guacamole, cut a small cross in the base of each tomato, place in a large bowl and cover with boiling water. Stand for 1 minute and then drain and slip off the skins. Quarter and de-seed one tomato and then finely dice the flesh. Mash the avocado flesh with the Quark and then mix in the diced tomato, half the red onion and half the lime juice, plus Tabasco and seasoning to taste.

3 To make the salsa, roughly chop the rest of the tomatoes. In a separate bowl, mix with the coriander and the remaining lime juice and red onion.

4 Serve the tortilla chips with the guacamole and salsa to dip into.

Tip... Smoked paprika has a wonderfully rich smoky flavour and is sold with the other spices in most major supermarkets. However, ordinary paprika can be used instead.

Lentil bolognese

Serves 4

424 calories per serving

Takes 20 minutes to prepare,
  30 minutes to cook

Ⓥ

❄ (sauce only)

**calorie controlled cooking
  spray**
1 onion, chopped finely
2 garlic cloves, chopped finely
200 g (7 oz) dried red lentils
2 carrots, peeled and chopped
**1 small butternut squash
  or ¼ pumpkin, peeled,
  de-seeded and diced**
4 celery sticks, chopped
400 g can chopped tomatoes
2 tablespoons tomato purée
1 teaspoon dried oregano
**600 ml (20 fl oz) vegetable
  stock**
225 g (8 oz) dried spaghetti
**salt and freshly ground black
  pepper**

*A new way with an old favourite that is easy to make, tasty
and satisfying.*

1 Spray a large, lidded, non stick saucepan with the cooking
spray and place on a medium heat. Add the onion and garlic
and cook until softened, about 5 minutes, adding a splash of
water if they start to stick.

2 Add the lentils, carrots, squash or pumpkin, celery, tomatoes,
tomato purée, oregano and stock. Stir, cover and simmer for
30 minutes. Check the seasoning.

3 Meanwhile, bring a saucepan of water to the boil, add
the pasta and cook for 8 minutes or according to the packet
instructions, until al dente. Drain and serve with the lentil
sauce.

Mushroom carbonara

Serves 4
377 calories per serving
Takes 25 minutes
Ⓥ

300 g (10½ oz) dried bucatini
25 g (1 oz) dried porcini
    mushrooms
150 ml (5 fl oz) boiling water
calorie controlled cooking
    spray
1 red onion, diced finely
1 garlic clove, crushed
300 g (10½ oz) baby portabello
    mushrooms, sliced
250 g (9 oz) Quark
2 egg yolks
1 tablespoon snipped fresh
    chives
salt and freshly ground black
    pepper

Bucatini is a thick spaghetti that is really good for creamy sauces, but you could use tagliatelle or spaghetti instead.

1 Bring a saucepan of water to the boil, add the pasta and cook for 7–8 minutes, or according to the packet instructions, until al dente.

2 Meanwhile, put the dried mushrooms into a small bowl and cover with the boiling water. Set aside.

3 Heat a non stick frying pan and spray with the cooking spray. Gently cook the onion for 3–4 minutes until softened. Add the garlic and portabello mushrooms and cook for a further 5 minutes. Remove from the heat.

4 Add the Quark, egg yolks and soaked mushrooms and their soaking liquid to the pan. Stir until smooth. Return to the heat and cook gently for 1 minute until slightly thickened.

5 Drain the pasta, return to the pan and stir in the cooked mushroom mixture and chives. Check the seasoning. Serve immediately in shallow bowls.

Baked couscous with tomatoes

Serves 4

222 calories per serving

Takes 10 minutes to prepare,
40 minutes to cook

Ⓥ

6 large tomatoes, halved

2 garlic cloves, sliced

1 tablespoon fresh thyme
leaves

2 red or green peppers,
de-seeded and cut into
large pieces

½ red onion, sliced finely

calorie controlled cooking
spray

125 g (4½ oz) dried couscous

300 ml (10 fl oz) vegetable
stock

150 g (5½ oz) low fat soft
cheese

salt and freshly ground black
pepper

*This one pot cooking really saves on the washing up.
Delicious with a mixed green salad tossed with a fat
free dressing.*

1 Preheat the oven to Gas Mark 6/200°C/fan oven 180°C.
Arrange the tomatoes, cut side up, in a deep roasting tin. Top
with the garlic and thyme. Scatter around the peppers and
onion and spray with the cooking spray. Bake for 20 minutes.

2 Carefully remove the tomatoes and set aside. Add the
couscous to the roasting tin and pour in the vegetable stock.
Carefully return the tomatoes, cut side up and continue to bake
in the oven for 10 minutes.

3 Dot the soft cheese over the tomatoes and couscous. Cook
for a further 5–10 minutes until the couscous is tender and
the stock has been absorbed. Season generously and serve
immediately.

Potato and leek pie

Serves 4

339 calories per serving

Takes 20 minutes to prepare,
   30–40 minutes to cook

Ⓥ

❄

calorie controlled cooking
   spray

3 large leeks, sliced thinly

2 garlic cloves, crushed

2 fresh thyme sprigs

250 g (9 oz) ready made
   shortcrust pastry

175 g (6 oz) potatoes, peeled
   and sliced thinly

salt and freshly ground black
   pepper

*This is a pastry tart filled with lightly caramelised leeks
and topped with thin and crispy potatoes. Serve with
steamed broccoli and carrots.*

1 Spray a large non stick frying pan with the cooking spray
and heat until hot. Add the leeks and cook over a medium heat
for 2–3 minutes. Reduce the heat, add the garlic, thyme and
2 tablespoons of water and continue cooking for 10 minutes.
The leeks should be very soft and slightly browned. Remove
from the heat and season.

2 Preheat the oven to Gas Mark 6/200°C/fan oven 180°C.

3 Roll out the pastry to about 28 x 22 cm (11 x 8½ inches).
Use a fork to mark the edges of the pastry to neaten it and
place it on a non stick baking tray. Spread the leeks evenly over
the pastry so that the fork markings create a border. Arrange
the thinly sliced potatoes on top and spray with the cooking
spray. Sprinkle with freshly ground black pepper. Bake for
30–40 minutes until the pastry and potatoes are golden and
cooked. Serve the pie warm.

Variation... Try making this pie with a mixture of leeks
and onions, using 2 leeks and 2 onions and cooking them
together in step 1.

Macaroni vegetable cheese

Serves 4
313 calories per serving
Takes 25 minutes

Ⓥ
❄

175 g (6 oz) dried macaroni

125 g (4½ oz) broccoli florets, cut into small pieces if large

2 carrots, peeled and cut into rounds

1 large leek, sliced

150 g (5½ oz) frozen petit pois

85 g (3 oz) half fat Cheddar cheese, grated

2 tablespoons fresh breadcrumbs

For the white sauce

1 teaspoon low fat spread

3 teaspoons plain flour

175 ml (6 fl oz) skimmed milk

1 teaspoon English mustard powder or Dijon mustard

½ vegetable stock cube

salt and freshly ground black pepper

Adding vegetables turns simple macaroni cheese into something a little more special.

1 Bring a saucepan of water to the boil, add the pasta and cook according to the packet instructions. Drain.

2 Meanwhile, bring another saucepan of water to the boil, cook the broccoli and carrots for 3 minutes and then add the leek and cook for another 1 minute. Add the petit pois to the pan and cook for a further minute. Drain thoroughly and set aside.

3 Meanwhile, for the white sauce, melt the low fat spread in a non stick saucepan, add the flour and stir for 1 minute. Gradually add the milk and whisk continuously until boiling. Stir in the mustard and stock cube, season and whisk well. Simmer, stirring, for 3 minutes until thickened.

4 Preheat the grill to medium-high. Add the white sauce to the drained pasta and vegetables and mix until combined. Pour into a 900 g (2 lb) heatproof dish and sprinkle over the cheese and breadcrumbs. Grill for 10 minutes or until the top is golden.

Spinach and potato gratin

Serves 4

450 calories per serving

Takes 40 minutes to prepare,
  40–50 minutes to cook

Ⓥ

750 g (1 lb 10 oz) potatoes,
  peeled and cut into 5 mm
  (¼ inch) thick slices
750 g (1 lb 10 oz) spinach,
  washed
2 teaspoons olive oil
250 g (9 oz) half fat mature
  Cheddar cheese, grated
250 g (12 oz) tomatoes, sliced
2 eggs
150 g (5½ oz) low fat natural
  yogurt
salt and freshly ground black
  pepper

A family favourite that is special enough for a dinner party too.

1 Preheat the oven to Gas Mark 4/180°C/fan oven 160°C. Bring a large saucepan of water to the boil, add the potatoes and cook for 5 minutes. Drain.

2 Pack the spinach into a very large lidded saucepan and add a little water. Cover and cook for 4–5 minutes, by which time the spinach will have wilted.

3 Drain the spinach well to make it as dry as possible, squeezing out any excess liquid with the back of a spoon.

4 Use the olive oil to grease a large, shallow, ovenproof dish. Layer half the potatoes over the base and season. Sprinkle with half the cheese and cover with the spinach. Top with the remaining potatoes and then the sliced tomatoes. Scatter the rest of the cheese evenly over the surface.

5 Beat the eggs and yogurt together and season. Pour this mixture carefully over the cheese and then bake for 40–50 minutes or until golden.

Veggie burgers

Serves 4
193 calories per serving
Takes 40 minutes
Ⓥ

These burgers are stuffed full of vegetables and served with a tasty Californian salsa.

400 g (14 oz) potatoes, peeled
    and quartered

500 g (1 lb 2 oz) mixed
    vegetables

calorie controlled cooking
    spray

2 leeks, chopped roughly

1 garlic clove, chopped

2 tablespoons soy sauce

1 tablespoon tomato purée

1 egg, beaten

a small bunch of fresh parsley,
    chopped

salt and freshly ground black
    pepper

For the salsa

100 g (3½ oz) cherry
    tomatoes, quartered

½ cucumber, diced finely

2 tablespoons tomato juice

1 small red onion, chopped
    finely

1 teaspoon horseradish sauce

1 Bring a large saucepan of water to the boil, add the potatoes and cook for 15 minutes until tender. Drain.

2 Meanwhile, bring a second saucepan of water to the boil, add the mixed vegetables and cook for 5 minutes. Drain.

3 Heat a non stick frying pan and spray with the cooking spray. Add the leeks and garlic and cook for 10 minutes until softened and golden, adding a splash of water if they start to stick.

4 Mash the potatoes and then add the vegetables, leeks and garlic, soy sauce, tomato purée, egg and parsley. Season and mix well.

5 Using wet hands, shape the mixture into eight burgers. Heat a large non stick frying pan and spray with the cooking spray. Fry the burgers for 4–5 minutes on each side.

6 Meanwhile, in a bowl, mix all the salsa ingredients together. Serve two burgers each with the salsa.

Mushroom pilaff

Serves 4

269 calories per serving

Takes 10 minutes to prepare
+ 10 minutes standing,
25 minutes to cook

Ⓥ

calorie controlled cooking
spray

300 g packet frozen exotic
mushrooms

1 red onion, sliced finely

1 tablespoon finely chopped
fresh sage

250 g (9 oz) dried brown
basmati rice

300 ml (10 fl oz) hot vegetable
stock

To serve

4 tablespoons 0% fat Greek
yogurt

½ teaspoon paprika

*Serve with a baby spinach salad drizzled with a fat
free dressing.*

1 Heat a deep, wide, lidded, non stick pan and spray with the
cooking spray. Cook the frozen mushrooms for 5 minutes and
then add the onion and sage and cook for 3–4 minutes until
starting to brown.

2 Stir in the rice and vegetable stock, cover tightly and cook
for 20–25 minutes until the rice is tender. Take off the heat and
leave to stand, covered, for 10 minutes. (Do not lift the lid.)

3 Divide between four warmed plates, topping each with
1 tablespoon of yogurt and a sprinkling of paprika.

Tip... If you can't find exotic frozen mushrooms then use
a selection of fresh ones such as porcini, oyster and
chestnut mushrooms.

Red pepper lasagne

Serves 4

305 calories per serving

Takes 30 minutes to prepare,
45 minutes to cook

Ⓥ

✳

4 red peppers, halved and
de-seeded

1 tablespoon olive oil

1 onion, chopped

1 garlic clove, crushed

175 g (6 oz) mushrooms,
sliced

400 g can chopped tomatoes

2 tablespoons chopped fresh
basil

25 g (1 oz) cornflour

300 ml (10 fl oz) skimmed milk

200 g (7 oz) low fat soft
cheese with garlic and herbs

6 no precook lasagne sheets

salt and freshly ground black
pepper

*Lasagne is not just for meat lovers – here is a wonderful
vegetarian version using red peppers.*

1 Preheat the grill to high, place the peppers skin side up on
a grill rack and grill until the skins are blackened. Transfer to a
plastic bag and leave until cool enough to handle. When cool,
peel away the skins and slice the flesh thinly.

2 Heat the olive oil in a non stick pan, add the onion and garlic
and cook until softened. Add the mushrooms and pepper strips
and cook for a further 5 minutes. Stir in the chopped tomatoes
and basil, season and simmer for 10 minutes.

3 Preheat the oven to Gas Mark 5/190°C/fan oven 170°C.
Mix the cornflour with a little of the milk to form a thin paste.
Heat the remaining milk until boiling and then pour over the
cornflour paste. Mix well and then return to the pan. Cook,
stirring, until the sauce thickens. Reduce the heat and simmer
for 5 minutes. Add the soft cheese and stir until the cheese
melts into the sauce.

4 To assemble, spoon half of the pepper mixture over the base
of a rectangular ovenproof dish and top with three lasagne
sheets. Drizzle with half of the sauce. Repeat the layers,
finishing with a layer of sauce.

5 Bake for 30 minutes until bubbling and golden on top. Serve
hot.

Polenta pizza pie

Serves 4
143 calories per serving
Takes 30 minutes
ⓥ

75 g (2¾ oz) dried instant
    polenta
25 g (1 oz) freshly grated
    Parmesan cheese
calorie controlled cooking
    spray
175 g (6 oz) cherry tomatoes,
    halved
110 g (4 oz) mushrooms,
    sliced
1 yellow pepper, de-seeded
    and sliced thinly
60 g (2 oz) light mozzarella
    cheese, drained and diced
salt and freshly ground black
    pepper

Polenta makes a good alternative to a dough base.

1 Preheat the oven to Gas Mark 6/200°C/fan oven 180°C.

2 Bring 400 ml (14 fl oz) of water to the boil in a large non stick saucepan. Tip in the polenta in a steady stream and stir until bubbling.

3 Reduce the heat and cook for 5 minutes, stirring occasionally, until well thickened. Remove from the heat and stir in 15 g (½ oz) of the Parmesan cheese. Season.

4 Pour the warm polenta into a 23 cm (9 inch) tart tin or ovenproof pan that has been lightly sprayed with the cooking spray. Alternatively, simply spread out to a circle on a sprayed baking tray.

5 Toss the vegetables in a bowl, season, spray with the cooking spray and pile them on to the polenta base. Cook on a high shelf in the oven for 10 minutes. Scatter the mozzarella and remaining Parmesan on top and cook for another 5 minutes until melted.

Vegetable noodles with ginger and soy

Serves 4
354 calories per serving
Takes 25 minutes
Ⓥ
❄

250 g (9 oz) dried medium egg
   noodles
1 tablespoon sunflower oil
2.5 cm (1 inch) fresh root
   ginger, grated
1 garlic clove, crushed
175 g (6 oz) carrots, peeled
   and cut into thin sticks
2 celery sticks, sliced
150 g (5½ oz) mushrooms,
   sliced
175 g (6 oz) courgettes, cut
   into sticks
100 g (3½ oz) mange tout
100 g (3½ oz) baby corn,
   halved
6 spring onions, sliced
3 tablespoons soy sauce
1 tablespoon medium sherry

A fast and colourful tasty supper dish.

1 Bring a saucepan of water to the boil, add the noodles and cook according to the packet instructions.

2 Heat the oil in a wok or large non stick frying pan and stir fry the ginger, garlic, carrots, celery, mushrooms, courgettes, mange tout and baby corn for 5 minutes.

3 Drain the noodles and toss into the vegetables with the spring onions, soy sauce and sherry. Cook for a further 2–3 minutes.

Tip... When you buy a piece of root ginger, keep what you don't use in the freezer so you can just grate a little as and when you need it.

Mushroom and pepper chilli

Serves 4

322 calories per serving

Takes 35 minutes to prepare,
20–30 minutes to cook

Ⓥ

❄

1 tablespoon vegetable oil

1 large onion, chopped

1 garlic clove, chopped

1 red chilli, de-seeded
   and chopped finely, or
   2 teaspoons chilli powder

1 large red or green pepper,
   de-seeded and chopped

250 g (9 oz) mushrooms,
   sliced

400 g can chopped tomatoes

2 tablespoons tomato purée

400 g can kidney beans,
   drained and rinsed

300 ml (10 fl oz) vegetable
   stock

1 teaspoon dried mixed herbs

2 tablespoons cornflour

salt and freshly ground black
   pepper

90 g (3¼ oz) taco chips, to
   serve

*Serve with a mixed salad of lettuce, tomatoes and
cucumber, as well as the taco chips, or replace them with
a 225 g (8 oz) potato, baked in its skin, per person.*

1 Heat the vegetable oil in a large, lidded, non stick pan. Add the onion, garlic, chilli and pepper and sauté for 3–4 minutes, until softened. Add the mushrooms and cook for another 2 minutes.

2 Pour in the tomatoes and stir in the tomato purée. Add the kidney beans, stock and herbs and bring to the boil. Reduce the heat and simmer, covered, for 20–30 minutes.

3 Blend the cornflour with a little water and add to the saucepan. Cook, stirring, for 2 minutes or until thickened. Check the seasoning.

4 Serve the chilli in warmed bowls, accompanied by the taco chips.

Veggie sausages with onion gravy

Serves 4
350 calories per serving
Takes 30 minutes
Ⓥ

1 red onion, cut into thin wedges

1 large garlic clove, sliced

1 fresh rosemary sprig, leaves only

8 x 53 g (1¾ oz) vegetarian Lincolnshire sausages

calorie controlled cooking spray

125 ml (4 fl oz) red wine

300 ml (10 fl oz) vegetable stock

1 tablespoon redcurrant jelly

3 teaspoons vegetarian gravy granules

2 x 400 g cans butter beans, drained and rinsed

salt and freshly ground black pepper

This truly is comfort food at its best. Serve with lots of tenderstem broccoli.

1 Preheat the oven to Gas Mark 6/200°C/fan oven 180°C. Put the onion, garlic, rosemary and sausages in a flameproof and ovenproof roasting tray and spray with the cooking spray. Cook in the oven for 20 minutes, stirring after 10 minutes.

2 Remove from the oven and transfer the sausages and onions to a warm plate to keep warm. Put the roasting tray on the hob and gently heat. Add the wine and bubble rapidly for 1 minute to deglaze the pan.

3 Stir in the stock and redcurrant jelly until combined. Bring to the boil, sprinkle over the gravy granules and stir until combined. Add the butter beans and seasoning and simmer for 1 minute until thickened and warmed through. Serve the sausages and onions with the butter beans and gravy on the side.

Roast vegetable quiche

Serves 4

206 calories per serving

Takes 15 minutes to prepare,
40–45 minutes to cook

Ⓥ

❄

1 green pepper, de-seeded and
sliced

1 red pepper, de-seeded and
sliced

1 yellow pepper, de-seeded
and sliced

1 red onion, sliced into eighths

4 shallots, quartered

4 carrots, peeled and sliced

calorie controlled cooking
spray

450 g (1 lb) potatoes, peeled
and cut into chunks

1 tablespoon horseradish
sauce

1 large egg

150 ml (5 fl oz) skimmed milk

2 tablespoons half fat Cheddar
cheese, grated

salt and freshly ground black
pepper

This is perfect for anyone who cannot eat pastry.

1 Preheat the oven to Gas Mark 7/220°C/fan oven 200°C.
Place all the vegetables apart from the potatoes in a roasting
tin. Season and spray them with the cooking spray. Toss
together and spray again. Roast for 20 minutes, until soft
and golden.

2 Meanwhile, bring a saucepan of water to the boil, add the
potatoes and cook for 15 minutes until tender. Drain and mash
them with the horseradish sauce and seasoning.

3 Line a 20 cm (8 inch) loose bottomed cake tin with non stick
baking parchment. Spoon in the mash and press down to form
a base. Bake in the oven for 10 minutes, until the potato has
formed a crust.

4 Pile the roasted vegetables on top of the potato base.

5 In a jug, beat together the egg and milk with some
seasoning. Pour the egg mixture over the vegetables and
then sprinkle over the grated cheese. Return to the oven
for a further 10–15 minutes, until the top is set and golden.
Serve hot or cold.

Curries, casseroles and stews

Aubergine madras

Serves 4

330 calories per serving

Takes 15 minutes to prepare,
25–30 minutes to cook

Ⓥ

1 teaspoon coriander seeds
½ teaspoon fennel seeds
½ teaspoon peppercorns
2 cloves
1 teaspoon chilli flakes
calorie controlled cooking
   spray
1 large onion, sliced
1 garlic clove, crushed
1 teaspoon grated fresh root
   ginger
2 aubergines, cut into chunks
2 tomatoes, chopped
200 ml (7 fl oz) low fat
   coconut milk
250 g (9 oz) dried basmati rice
salt and freshly ground black
   pepper

*Madras has come to be known as a very hot curry in this
country – this recipe is no exception.*

1 Heat a non stick frying pan over a medium heat and add
the coriander and fennel seeds, peppercorns, cloves and chilli
flakes. Heat until they start to darken and you can smell the
aroma. Leave to cool and then grind in a coffee grinder or with
a pestle and mortar.

2 Spray a large, lidded, non stick pan with the cooking spray,
add the onion and garlic and cook for 4–5 minutes until starting
to soften.

3 Add the ginger, aubergines and tomatoes and stir well
before adding the spice mixture. Stir well again and then pour
in the coconut milk. Bring to the boil, cover and simmer for
10 minutes.

4 Meanwhile, bring a saucepan of water to the boil, add the
rice and cook according to the packet instructions.

5 Uncover the curry and cook for another 10–15 minutes, until
the aubergine is tender and the juices have started to thicken
slightly. Check the seasoning and serve with the cooked
basmati rice.

Winter vegetable korma

Serves 4
305 calories per serving
Takes 10 minutes to prepare,
  20 minutes to cook

Ⓥ
❄ (after step 2)

1 tablespoon vegetable oil

2 large onions, sliced

2 garlic cloves, crushed

1 tablespoon ground cumin

1 tablespoon ground coriander

1 teaspoon turmeric

1 teaspoon ground ginger or 4 cm (1½ inch) fresh root ginger, grated

1 tablespoon plain flour

450 ml (16 fl oz) vegetable stock

1 tablespoon tomato purée

225 g (8 oz) carrots, peeled and sliced

225 g (8 oz) parsnips, peeled and chopped

275 g (9½ oz) cauliflower florets

425 g can chick peas, drained and rinsed

110 g (4 oz) button mushrooms, halved

4 tablespoons low fat natural yogurt

salt

2 tablespoons chopped fresh coriander or parsley, to garnish

Korma is one of the mildest (and creamiest) of curries. Enjoy this dish with either 60 g (2 oz) of dried rice per person, cooked according to the packet instructions, or ½ medium naan bread per person.

1 Heat the oil in a large, lidded, non stick saucepan, add the onions and cook gently for 5 minutes, until softened and golden. Add the garlic and stir in the ground spices, including the ground or fresh ginger. Cook for a minute. Sprinkle on the flour and cook for a further minute

2 Blend in the vegetable stock until smooth and then add the tomato purée, carrots and parsnips. Bring to the boil, cover and simmer for 10 minutes. Add the cauliflower, chick peas and mushrooms and simmer for a further 10 minutes.

3 Season with salt, take the pan off the heat and lightly swirl in the yogurt. Serve garnished with the chopped herbs.

Tips... For a hotter curry, add ½–1 teaspoon of chilli powder in step 1 with the other spices.

For a quick korma, replace all the vegetables with frozen mixed vegetables.

Winter casserole with herb dumplings

Serves 4

405 calories per serving

Takes 35 minutes to prepare,
15–20 minutes to cook

Ⓥ

300 g (10½ oz) parsnips, peeled and cut into 1 cm (½ inch) dice

2 teaspoons olive oil

calorie controlled cooking spray

8 shallots, cut in half lengthways

2 garlic cloves, sliced finely

350 g (12 oz) carrots, peeled and sliced thinly, diagonally

350 g (12 oz) turnips, peeled and cut into 2.5 cm (1 inch) chunks

1 tablespoon cornflour

200 ml (7 fl oz) cider

200 g (7 oz) button mushrooms

350 ml (12 fl oz) vegetable stock

1 bay leaf

salt and freshly ground black pepper

For the dumplings

125 g (4½ oz) self raising flour

50 g (1¾ oz) half fat Cheddar cheese, grated

50 g (1¾ oz) low fat spread

a small bunch of fresh parsley, chopped finely

A delicious, warming and filling casserole – perfect on a cold and frosty winter's day.

1 Preheat the oven to its highest setting and toss the parsnips with the olive oil and seasoning. Roast on a non stick baking tray for 20–25 minutes, until golden brown. Keep warm.

2 Meanwhile, heat a large, lidded, non stick saucepan and spray with the cooking spray. Add the shallots and garlic and fry for 4 minutes until softened, adding a splash of water if they start to stick.

3 Add the carrots and turnips and stir fry for a further 5 minutes. In a small bowl, mix the cornflour with 2 tablespoons of the cider. Add the mushrooms, stock, remaining cider and bay leaf to the pan. Cover and cook for 5 minutes.

4 Meanwhile, make the dumplings by mixing the ingredients together, with seasoning, reserving a little chopped parsley. Add about 1 tablespoon of water to make a soft dough. Form into about 16 walnut sized balls and set aside.

5 Add the cornflour paste and seasoning to the stew and bring back to the boil, stirring occasionally. Once thickened, add the dumplings carefully so that they are about three quarters immersed. Cover and simmer for 15–20 minutes, until the dumplings have risen.

6 Scatter the parsnips over the top, with the reserved parsley, and serve.

Sweet potato saag aloo

Serves 4
222 calories per serving
Takes 25 minutes
Ⓥ
❄

700 g (1 lb 9 oz) sweet
  potatoes, peeled and cubed
calorie controlled cooking
  spray
3 cloves
2 teaspoons mustard seeds
2 teaspoons cumin seeds
1–2 long red chillies,
  de-seeded and cut into long
  strips
3 large garlic cloves, chopped
5 cm (2 inches) fresh root
  ginger, chopped finely
400 g (14 oz) spinach, washed
  and shredded
4 tablespoons low fat natural
  yogurt
salt and freshly ground black
  pepper

*Saag aloo is usually made with regular potatoes; the sweet
variety add an extra dimension.*

1 Bring a saucepan of water to the boil, add the sweet potatoes
and cook for 10–12 minutes until tender. Drain well.

2 Spray a large non stick frying pan with the cooking spray and
fry the cloves, mustard seeds and cumin seeds until they start
to pop and smell aromatic.

3 Add the chillies, garlic, ginger and spinach and stir fry for
2 minutes until the spinach has wilted. Stir in the sweet potato,
3 tablespoons of water and the yogurt. Season well and cook
for 1–2 minutes, stirring frequently until combined.

Lentil curry with crispy onions

Serves 4
185 calories per serving
Takes 50 minutes
Ⓥ
❄

Red lentils cook quickly and are perfect for this spicy dish.

**calorie controlled cooking
  spray**
**2 onions, 1 chopped finely
  and 1 sliced**
3 garlic cloves, chopped
**2.5 cm (1 inch) fresh root
  ginger, chopped finely**
2 teaspoons cumin seeds
2 teaspoons ground coriander
1 teaspoon hot chilli powder
1 teaspoon turmeric
5 curry leaves
1 carrot, peeled and chopped
**3 string beans, trimmed and
  sliced diagonally**
140 g (5 oz) dried red lentils
**850 ml (1½ pints) vegetable
  stock**
**salt and freshly ground black
  pepper**

1 Spray a large, lidded, non stick saucepan with the cooking spray, add the chopped onion and cook for 6 minutes until softened and beginning to turn golden. Add the garlic, ginger and spices (except the curry leaves) and cook for 1 minute, adding a splash of water if they start to stick.

2 Stir in the curry leaves, carrot, string beans and lentils. Cook for 1 minute until everything is coated with the spice mixture and then pour in the stock. Bring to the boil, reduce the heat and simmer, partially covered, for 20–25 minutes, stirring occasionally, until the lentils are very tender. Season to taste.

3 Meanwhile, spray a non stick frying pan with the cooking spray and fry the sliced onion for 10 minutes until crisp – you may need to add a little water.

4 Serve the curry topped with the fried sliced onions.

Sweet pumpkin and peanut curry

Serves 4

275 calories per serving

Takes 30 minutes to prepare,
20 minutes to cook

Ⓥ

2 teaspoons vegetable oil

4 garlic cloves, crushed

4 shallots, chopped finely

2 teaspoons red or green Thai
curry paste

600 ml (20 fl oz) vegetable
stock

2 kaffir lime leaves, torn

2.5 cm (1 inch) fresh root
ginger, chopped finely

450 g (1 lb) pumpkin, peeled,
de-seeded and cubed

200 g (7 oz) sweet potatoes,
peeled and cubed

100 g (3½ oz) mushrooms,
sliced

100 ml (3½ fl oz) low fat
coconut milk

50 g (1¾ oz) roasted peanuts,
chopped

3 tablespoons soy sauce

a small bunch of fresh
coriander, chopped

*Serve this hearty curry with 60 g (2 oz) of dried basmati rice
per person, cooked according to the packet instructions.*

1 Heat the oil in a large non stick pan, add the garlic and
shallots and cook for 10 minutes, until softened and golden,
adding a splash of water if they start to stick.

2 Add the curry paste and stir fry for 30 seconds. Add the stock,
lime leaves, ginger, pumpkin and sweet potatoes. Bring to the
boil and simmer for 20 minutes or until the potatoes are cooked.

3 Add the mushrooms and simmer for a further 5 minutes
before removing from the heat and stirring in the coconut milk,
peanuts, soy sauce and coriander. Serve.

Vegetable balti

Serves 4

238 calories per serving

Takes 20 minutes to prepare,
  30 minutes to cook

calorie controlled cooking spray

2 large onions, sliced finely

4 garlic cloves, crushed

2.5 cm (1 inch) fresh root ginger, chopped finely

1 small red chilli, de-seeded and chopped (optional)

½ teaspoon cumin seeds, crushed

1 teaspoon coriander seeds, crushed

1 tablespoon garam masala

200 g (7 oz) potatoes, peeled and diced

4 carrots, peeled and chopped

1 small cauliflower, broken into florets

400 g can chopped tomatoes

300 ml (10 fl oz) vegetable stock

200 g (7 oz) green beans, trimmed and chopped

150 g (5½ oz) low fat natural yogurt

salt and freshly ground black pepper

a small bunch of fresh coriander, chopped (optional)

Great flavours and none of the fat associated with a takeaway equivalent. This curry keeps well in the fridge for a few days or could be made in advance and frozen.

1 Heat a large non stick frying pan and spray with the cooking spray. Add the onions and stir fry for 5 minutes, adding a splash of water if they start to stick. Mix in the garlic, ginger, chilli, if using, and spices, season and cook for a further 2 minutes.

2 Add the potatoes, carrots, cauliflower, tomatoes and stock, stir together and bring to the boil. Turn down the heat and then simmer for 20 minutes.

3 Add the beans and simmer a further 5 minutes or until the sauce is thick.

4 Remove the pan from the heat and allow to cool a little before stirring in the yogurt and fresh coriander, if using, and then serve.

Vegetable and haricot bean bake

Serves 4

413 calories per serving

Takes 20 minutes to prepare,
1 hour to cook

*Roast seasonal vegetables to bring out their flavour and
then mix them with haricot beans and tomatoes to make a
tasty casserole.*

1 Preheat the oven to Gas Mark 6/200°C/180°C.

2 Tip the squash, parsnips, carrots and courgettes into a large
ovenproof baking dish. Season and then sprinkle with the olive
oil and cumin seeds, if using. Toss together and roast for
30 minutes, turning the vegetables after 15 minutes.

3 Remove the baking dish from the oven and reduce the
temperature to Gas Mark 4/180°C/fan oven 160°C.

4 Add the haricot beans, tomatoes and vegetable stock to the
baking dish. Blend the cornflour with a little cold water and stir
in. Return to the oven and bake for 20 minutes.

5 Spread the slices of French stick with the low fat spread and
garlic purée. Arrange them on top of the vegetables and then
bake for another 5–6 minutes, until crispy and brown.

6 Serve the vegetable bake by topping each portion with two
pieces of garlic bread.

450 g (1 lb) butternut squash,
peeled, de-seeded and thinly
sliced

225 g (8 oz) parsnips, peeled
and sliced

2 large carrots, scrubbed and
thinly sliced

2 courgettes, thinly sliced

2 tablespoons olive oil

1 teaspoon cumin seeds
(optional)

420 g can haricot beans,
drained and rinsed

400 g can chopped tomatoes
with herbs

150 ml (5 fl oz) hot vegetable
stock

2 tablespoons cornflour

8 x 15 g (½ oz) slices French
stick

4 teaspoons low fat spread

2–3 teaspoons garlic purée

salt and freshly ground black
pepper

Spicy vegetable tagine

Serves 4
247 calories per serving
Takes 45 minutes
☉
❄

calorie controlled cooking
   spray
2 onions, chopped
3 garlic cloves, chopped finely
600 g (1 lb 5 oz) butternut
   squash, peeled, de-seeded
   and cut into 1 cm (½ inch)
   dice
1 tablespoon ground cumin
1 tablespoon ground coriander
1 teaspoon cinnamon
1 teaspoon hot chilli powder
1 teaspoon turmeric
2 x 400 g cans chopped
   tomatoes
2 teaspoons tomato purée
2 courgettes, sliced thickly
400 g can chick peas, drained
   and rinsed
400 g can apricots in natural
   juice, drained and sliced
salt and freshly ground black
   pepper
2 tablespoons fresh coriander,
   to garnish

*Serve with 60 g (2 oz) of dried basmati rice per person,
cooked according to the packet instructions.*

1 Spray a large, lidded, non stick saucepan with the cooking
spray and fry the onions for 8–10 minutes or until soft, adding
a splash of water if they start to stick.

2 Spray with more cooking spray, add the garlic and fry for
1 minute. Add the squash to the pan with the spices and cook
for another minute.

3 Add the tomatoes, tomato purée and 150 ml (5 fl oz) of
water. Bring to the boil, reduce the heat and simmer, covered,
for 10 minutes.

4 Stir in the courgettes, chick peas and apricots. Season and
cook, partially covered, for 10–15 minutes until the vegetables
are tender. Add a little extra water if the tagine appears dry.

5 Serve sprinkled with the fresh coriander.

Cook ahead Deep South stew

Serves 1

232 calories per serving

Takes 15 minutes to prepare,
15–20 minutes to cook

Ⓥ

A rich warming stew based on the flavours popular in the southern states of America. Serve with fresh greens such as broccoli.

1 Spray a large, lidded, non stick saucepan with the cooking spray, add the onion and garlic and cook for 5 minutes until softened, adding a splash of water if they start to stick.

2 Add the carrots, okra or green beans, baby corn, tomato purée, tomatoes, spices, kidney beans, stock and seasoning.

3 Bring to the boil, cover and simmer gently for 15–20 minutes or until all the vegetables are tender and the sauce is rich and thick.

calorie controlled cooking spray

1 small onion, sliced finely

1 garlic clove, crushed

50 g (1¾ oz) baby carrots, scrubbed and halved lengthways if large

50 g (1¾ oz) okra or green beans

50 g (1¾ oz) baby corn, halved lengthways if large

1 tablespoon tomato purée

200 g can chopped tomatoes

½ teaspoon chilli flakes

½ teaspoon ground cinnamon

200 g can kidney beans, drained and rinsed

200 ml (7 fl oz) vegetable stock

salt and freshly ground black pepper

Provençal Quorn bake

Serves 4
270 calories per serving
Takes 30 minutes
Ⓥ

Quorn makes a wonderful meat substitute in this filling tasty dish.

800 g (1 lb 11 oz) potatoes, peeled and cut into 2 cm (¾ inch) dice
1 vegetable stock cube
calorie controlled cooking spray
8 x 51 g (1¾ oz) frozen Quorn pieces
2 garlic cloves, crushed
400 g can chopped tomatoes
1 heaped teaspoon dried herbes de Provence or dried mixed herbs
salt and freshly ground black pepper

1 Preheat the oven to Gas Mark 7/220°C/fan oven 200°C.

2 Bring a large lidded saucepan of water to the boil and add the potatoes and stock cube. Bring back to the boil, cover and simmer for 4 minutes. Drain, reserving 200 ml (7 fl oz) of the cooking water, and then shake up the potatoes lightly to roughen the edges (this helps to crisp them up).

3 Meanwhile, spray a non stick frying pan with the cooking spray and brown the Quorn pieces for 1½ minutes. Transfer to an ovenproof baking dish.

4 Add the garlic to the frying pan and cook for 20–30 seconds, without burning, then tip in the tomatoes, herbs and reserved cooking water. Season, bring to a simmer and pour over the Quorn pieces in the dish.

5 Scatter the potatoes on top of the Quorn and sauce and lightly spray with the cooking spray. Bake in the oven for 18 minutes until the potatoes are crisp on top.

Pumpkin stew

Serves 4
251 calories per serving
Takes 40 minutes
Ⓥ

250 g (9 oz) potatoes, peeled
and cut into chunks

300 g (10½ oz) pumpkin,
peeled, de-seeded and cut
into chunks

calorie controlled cooking
spray

1 red onion, cut into wedges

2 garlic cloves, chopped

1 red chilli, de-seeded and
diced (optional)

1 red pepper, de-seeded and
sliced

198 g can sweetcorn, drained

400 g can butter beans,
drained and rinsed

400 g can chopped tomatoes

1 vegetable stock cube,
crumbled

75 g (2¾ oz) Feta cheese,
crumbled, to serve

*It's best to make this wonderfully colourful stew in the
autumn when there are plenty of different pumpkins to
choose from. If you prefer it not to be spicy, omit the chilli.*

1 Bring a large saucepan of water to the boil, add the potatoes
and pumpkin and cook for 10 minutes. Drain and set aside.

2 Lightly spray a large non stick saucepan with the cooking
spray and heat until hot. Add the onion and stir fry for 5 minutes.
Add the garlic, chilli, if using, and pepper. Cook for a further
minute.

3 Add the potatoes, pumpkin, sweetcorn, butter beans,
tomatoes and stock cube. Stir to mix, adding 125 ml (4 fl oz)
of water. Simmer gently for 10 minutes until the vegetables
are tender. Serve sprinkled with the Feta cheese.

Tip... If pumpkin is not in season, you can use butternut
squash instead.

Roasted ragoût with borlotti beans

Serves 4

128 calories per serving

Takes 10 minutes to prepare, 55 minutes to cook

Ⓥ

1 small courgette, cut into chunks

1 yellow pepper, de-seeded and sliced

1 red pepper, de-seeded and sliced

2 red onions, cut into wedges

4 garlic cloves, unpeeled

1 fresh rosemary sprig

calorie controlled cooking spray

10 vine ripened tomatoes

410 g can borlotti beans, drained and rinsed

150 ml (5 fl oz) vegetable stock

salt and freshly ground black pepper

a handful of fresh basil leaves, to garnish

This is a very easy, all in one pan recipe.

1 Preheat the oven to Gas Mark 6/200°C/fan oven 180°C.

2 Place the courgette, peppers, onions, garlic and rosemary in a large roasting tin. Spray with the cooking spray and cook in the oven for 30 minutes until beginning to char.

3 Add the tomatoes and cook for a further 15 minutes until they are soft.

4 Stir in the borlotti beans and stock, splitting some of the tomatoes so that they form a sauce. Cover with foil and cook for a further 10 minutes until hot.

5 Season and garnish with the basil leaves before serving.

Variation... Replace the borlotti beans with a drained 410 g can of green lentils.

Italian chick pea and pasta stew

Serves 4
305 calories per serving
Takes 30 minutes

175 g (6 oz) dried farfalle

calorie controlled cooking spray

1 large onion, chopped

1 celery stick, sliced

2 carrots, peeled and diced

850 ml (1½ pints) vegetable stock

400 g can chopped tomatoes

1 tablespoon tomato purée

2 bay leaves

2 fresh rosemary sprigs

400 g can chick peas, drained and rinsed

250 g (9 oz) spinach, washed, thick stalks removed and leaves sliced

salt and freshly ground black pepper

This hearty stew makes a filling and healthy complete meal.

1 Bring a saucepan of water to the boil, add the pasta and cook according to the packet instructions. Drain.

2 Meanwhile, spray a large non stick saucepan with the cooking spray and add the onion, celery and carrots. Cook for 5 minutes, stirring regularly.

3 Add the stock, tomatoes, tomato purée, bay leaves and rosemary and bring to the boil. Reduce the heat and simmer for 5 minutes. Add the chick peas and cook for another 10 minutes. Remove the rosemary sprigs and bay leaves.

4 Stir in the spinach and cooked pasta and cook for a final 2 minutes. Season. Serve in large bowls.

Savoury vegetable crumble

Serves 4

319 calories per serving

Takes 25 minutes to prepare,
40 minutes to cook

Ⓥ

❄

1 teaspoon vegetable oil
1 tablespoon soy sauce
2 leeks, sliced
2 carrots, peeled and diced
225 g (8 oz) button
    mushrooms, quartered
175 g (6 oz) baby corn, halved
100 g (3½ oz) frozen peas
275 g can Weight Watchers
    from Heinz Vegetable Soup
salt and freshly ground black
    pepper

For the crumble
100 g (3½ oz) plain flour
25 g (1 oz) rolled oats
50 g (1¾ oz) low fat spread
50 g (1¾ oz) reduced fat Red
    Leicester cheese, grated

An unusual topping turns this veggie bake into something special.

1 Heat the vegetable oil and soy sauce in a large lidded saucepan and add the leeks, carrots, mushrooms, baby corn and peas. Cover and cook over a low heat for 5 minutes, stirring halfway through.

2 Stir in the soup, season to taste and heat through. Transfer to a shallow ovenproof dish.

3 Preheat the oven to Gas Mark 5/190°C/fan oven 170°C.

4 For the crumble, sift the flour into a mixing bowl and stir in the oats. Rub in the low fat spread using your fingertips and then stir in the cheese. Sprinkle over the vegetable mixture and bake for 30 minutes, until the topping is golden and crunchy. Serve hot.

Variation... Try adding different flavours of soup such as tomato or mushroom.

Entertaining

Mini filo pastries

Serves 8 (2 each)

92 calories per serving

Takes 15 minutes to prepare,
15 minutes to cook

Ⓥ

calorie controlled cooking spray

1 large carrot, peeled and diced

2 banana shallots or 4 round shallots, chopped finely

1 large red or green pepper, de-seeded and diced

4 x 15 g (½ oz) filo pastry sheets, measuring 30 x 40 cm (12 x 16 inches)

6 x 30 g (1¼ oz) sun-dried tomatoes, reconstituted according to the packet instructions

2 tablespoons sun-dried tomato paste

60 g (2 oz) light mozzarella cheese, drained and cut into chunks

You could make these canapés ahead of time and warm through in the oven before serving.

1 Preheat the oven to Gas Mark 6/200°C/fan oven 180°C. Spray a non stick frying pan with the cooking spray and heat until hot. Add the carrot, shallots and pepper and cook for 5 minutes until softened. Add a splash of water if they start to stick.

2 Spray each sheet of filo pastry with the cooking spray and cut each sheet into eight rectangles. In a 16 hole non stick mini muffin tin (see Tip), place two layered rectangles at an angle in each hole. Press down gently to the bottom.

3 Cut the soaked tomatoes into thin strips and stir into the carrot mixture with the sun-dried tomato paste. Fill the pastry cases with the mixture and top each with a piece of mozzarella. Bake for 12–15 minutes until golden. Serve warm.

Tip... If you don't have a mini muffin tin, place the filo rectangles in small cake papers in a bun tin to bake.

Spinach and soft cheese roulade

Serves 6

123 calories per serving

Takes 35 minutes +
30 minutes cooling

Ⓥ

200 g (7 oz) baby spinach
leaves, washed

a pinch of ground nutmeg

25 g (1 oz) low fat spread

25 g (1 oz) plain flour

200 ml (7 fl oz) skimmed milk

3 eggs, separated

125 g (4½ oz) low fat soft
cheese with garlic and herbs

salt and freshly ground black
pepper

*Roulades have a similar mixture to soufflés and will puff
up in the oven; as it cools the roulade will shrink again, but
this is quite normal.*

1 Place the spinach in a lidded saucepan with the nutmeg and
2 tablespoons of water. Cover and cook for 2–3 minutes until
wilted. Drain, squeeze out any excess water and chop finely.

2 Melt the low fat spread in a medium saucepan and stir in
the flour. Gradually add the milk and cook, whisking until you
have a thick smooth sauce. Stir in the chopped spinach and
seasoning and then whisk in the egg yolks.

3 Preheat the oven to Gas Mark 5/190°C/fan oven 170°C. Line
a 23 x 28 cm (9 x 11 inch) Swiss roll tin with non stick baking
parchment.

4 In a clean, grease-free bowl, whisk the egg whites until they
form soft peaks. Fold them into the spinach mixture, turn it all
into the prepared tin and bake for 12 minutes.

5 Turn the roulade out on to a clean sheet of non stick baking
parchment and peel away the parchment lining the base. Roll
up the roulade like a Swiss roll, using the clean sheet of baking
parchment to guide it along. Allow it to cool for 30 minutes.

6 Mash the soft cheese to soften it slightly. Carefully unroll the
roulade, spread it with the soft cheese and then re-roll. Serve
cut into slices.

Variation... If you aren't keen on spinach, try using
watercress instead. You will only need 150 g (5½ oz)
of watercress, with the tough stalks removed.

Greek stuffed tomatoes and peppers

Serves 2

634 calories per serving

Takes 25 minutes to prepare,
  45 minutes to cook

Ⓥ

115 g (4 oz) dried brown rice

calorie controlled cooking
  spray

2 large onions, chopped finely

2 garlic cloves, chopped

50 g (1¾ oz) currants

1 tablespoon toasted pine nut
  kernels

grated zest and juice of a
  lemon

4 large tomatoes

4 large peppers

2 tablespoons fresh
  breadcrumbs

salt and freshly ground black
  pepper

To serve

a small bunch of fresh flat leaf
  parsley, chopped

a small bunch of fresh
  coriander or mint, chopped

*The practice of stuffing vegetables is very popular all over
the Mediterranean but especially in Greece.*

1 Bring a large saucepan of water to the boil, add the rice and
cook for 30 minutes or according to the packet instructions.
Drain and place in a large bowl.

2 Meanwhile, heat a non stick frying pan, spray with the
cooking spray and sauté the onions and garlic for 4 minutes,
adding a splash of water if they start to stick. Add to the rice in
the bowl.

4 Add the currants, pine nut kernels, lemon zest and lemon
juice to the bowl. Season and toss together.

5 Preheat the oven to Gas Mark 4/180°C/fan oven 160°C. Cut
a round from the top of each tomato, spoon out the flesh with
a teaspoon and add to the stuffing mix. Cut off the top of each
pepper and discard the seeds. Place the tomatoes and peppers
side by side, packed closely together in an ovenproof baking
dish.

6 Spoon the stuffing into the peppers and tomatoes, sprinkle
over the breadcrumbs and replace the lids.

7 Bake for 15 minutes and serve with the herbs as a garnish.

Variation... You could also stuff courgettes or aubergines
with the same mixture, adding chopped dried apricots or
prunes instead of the currants and using fresh basil or
marjoram instead of the parsley or mint.

Roast vegetable pilaff

Serves 6
296 calories per serving
Takes 20 minutes to prepare,
  45 minutes to cook
Ⓥ

500 g (1 lb 2 oz) parsnips,
  peeled and cut into wedges
300 g (10½ oz) carrots, peeled
  and chopped roughly
300 g (10½ oz) butternut
  squash, peeled, de-seeded
  and chopped roughly
6 shallots, halved
1 head of garlic, broken into
  whole cloves
1 tablespoon soy sauce
1 tablespoon balsamic vinegar
a few fresh rosemary sprigs,
  one reserved for the garnish,
  leaves chopped roughly
calorie controlled cooking
  spray
salt and freshly ground black
  pepper

For the rice
300 g (10½ oz) dried brown rice
a pinch of saffron
850 ml (1½ pints) vegetable
  stock

Serve with a mixed salad.

1 Preheat the oven to Gas Mark 4/180°C/fan oven 160°C.
Place all the vegetables in a large roasting tin with the garlic,
soy sauce, balsamic vinegar and chopped rosemary. Spray with
the cooking spray, season, toss together and spray again. Roast
on the top shelf of the oven for 45 minutes or until tender.

2 Meanwhile, place the rice in a lidded flameproof and
ovenproof casserole. Stir the saffron into the stock, pour this
over the rice and stir. Bring to the boil and stir well. Cover and
cook in the oven on a lower shelf for 40 minutes.

3 Remove the casserole from the oven, stir in the roasted
vegetables and then return the casserole to the oven for a
further 5 minutes, or until the rice is tender. The pilaff should
be slightly moist, so if the rice dries out too quickly add a little
more stock or water. Garnish with the reserved rosemary sprig.

Curried cauliflower fritters

Serves 4

99 calories per serving

Takes 30 minutes +
30 minutes standing
(optional)

Ⓥ

200 g (7 oz) cauliflower,
broken into small florets

3 tablespoons plain flour

1 teaspoon curry powder

1 egg, separated

3 tablespoons skimmed milk

calorie controlled cooking
spray

salt and freshly ground black
pepper

For the dip

5 cm (2 inches) fresh root
ginger, grated finely

3 tablespoons soy sauce

3 tablespoons rice vinegar

*These delicious little fritters are great as a starter, or to
serve at a buffet.*

1 Bring a saucepan of water to the boil, add the cauliflower
florets and blanch for a few minutes, until just tender. Drain,
reserving 3 tablespoons of the cooking liquid.

2 Meanwhile place the flour in a bowl with the curry powder
and seasoning. Stir in the egg yolk and milk, mixing thoroughly,
and then add the cauliflower and reserved cooking liquid and
fold gently together. Set aside for about 30 minutes, if you have
time.

3 Make the dip by mixing all the dip ingredients together in a
small bowl.

4 In a clean, grease-free bowl, whisk the egg white until stiff
peaks form and then gently fold into the cauliflower batter with
a large metal spoon.

5 Heat a large non stick frying pan and spray with the cooking
spray. Drop in tablespoonfuls of the batter, cooking five or
six fritters at the same time for 3–4 minutes. Flip over with
a palette knife and cook the other side for 3–4 minutes, until
golden brown. Keep warm on a plate while you cook the
remaining batter and then serve with the dip.

Mulled Quorn pot

Serves 4

127 calories per serving

Takes 15 minutes to prepare, 15 minutes to cook

Ⓥ

2 teaspoons Sichaun peppercorns

1 tablespoon fresh thyme leaves

4 x 51 g (1¾ oz) Quorn fillets

calorie controlled cooking spray

1 red onion, sliced finely

2 red eating apples, peeled, cored and each cut into eighths

½ x 810 g jar sauerkraut, drained

2 teaspoons vegetable gravy granules

300 ml (10 fl oz) hot vegetable stock

1 bag mulled wine spices

Sauerkraut is pickled cabbage and can be found with the pickled gherkins and onions in most supermarkets.

1 Crush the peppercorns lightly with a pestle and mortar. Put the crushed peppercorns and thyme on to a plate and press the Quorn fillets into the mixture to coat one side.

2 Spray a large, lidded, non stick saucepan with the cooking spray and cook the Quorn fillets for 5 minutes until brown. Remove and set aside.

3 Spray the pan again with the cooking spray and cook the onion and apples for 3–4 minutes until starting to brown. Add the sauerkraut, gravy granules and stock and stir lightly until the granules have dissolved. Empty the spices out of the mulled wine spice bag and into the pan, stirring until mixed.

4 Return the Quorn fillets, nestling them into the cabbage. Bring to the boil, cover tightly and simmer for 15 minutes until the apples are tender and the juices have thickened. Serve immediately.

Broad bean and mint risotto

Serves 4

350 calories per serving

Takes 15 minutes to prepare,
  30 minutes to cook

Ⓨ
❄

1 tablespoon olive oil

4 shallots, thinly sliced

1 garlic clove, crushed

225 g (8 oz) dried risotto rice

30 ml (1 fl oz) vermouth
  (optional)

700 ml (1¼ pints) vegetable
  stock

350 g (12 oz) shelled broad
  beans

25 g (1 oz) Parmesan cheese,
  grated

2 tablespoons chopped fresh
  mint

Peeling the broad beans is time consuming but the end result with the bright green beans makes it really worthwhile. Vermouth lifts the taste of risotto from super to sublime so do try it for a treat.

1 Heat the olive oil in a large non stick frying pan and cook the shallots and garlic for 2–3 minutes, until just beginning to soften. Add the rice and stir well. Cook for a further 2–3 minutes.

2 Stir in the vermouth, if using. Gradually add the stock a little at a time, waiting for what you add to be absorbed by the rice before adding more.

3 Meanwhile, bring a small saucepan of water to the boil, add the broad beans and cook for 5 minutes. Drain, rinse with cold water to cool rapidly and remove and discard the skins to reveal the bright green beans.

4 As you are adding the last of the stock, toss in the broad beans, Parmesan and mint. Continue cooking until the rice is creamy and tender. A successful risotto should also be a bit sloppy. It should take about 20 minutes in all. Serve at once.

Tip... If you're freezing this, you may want to add some extra stock as you heat it through.

Variation... To save time, you could use frozen peas instead of broad beans.

Savoury tarte tatin

Serves 4

271 calories per serving

Takes 30 minutes to prepare,
   20 minutes to cook

Ⓥ

❄

175 g (6 oz) courgettes, sliced

1 red onion, cut into thin
   wedges

225 g (8 oz) open cup
   mushrooms, halved

1 garlic clove, crushed

a fresh rosemary sprig, leaves
   chopped

1 tablespoon olive oil

1 teaspoon balsamic vinegar

175 g (6 oz) small tomatoes,
   halved

175 g (6 oz) puff pastry

2 teaspoons plain flour, for
   rolling

salt and freshly ground black
   pepper

*The colourful topping of this upside down tart will begin to
caramelise as it cooks, giving it a lovely thick glaze.*

1 Preheat the oven to Gas Mark 6/200°C/fan oven 180°C.
Mix together the courgettes, red onion, mushrooms, garlic,
rosemary, olive oil, balsamic vinegar and seasoning. Arrange
them on a non stick baking tray lined with non stick baking
parchment and roast for 15 minutes.

2 Remove the vegetables from the oven. Arrange all
the vegetables, including the tomatoes, on the base of a
20 cm (8 inch) non stick frying pan or cake tin (see Tip).

3 Roll out the pastry on a lightly floured surface to make a
23 cm (9 inch) circle. Lay the pastry over the vegetables,
tucking in the edges all the way round. Bake the tart in the
oven for 20 minutes, until the pastry is well risen and golden.

4 Carefully run a round bladed knife around the edge of the
pan or tin. Put a large plate over the top and turn the pan or tin
upside down, so that the tart drops on to the plate. Cut the tart
into quarters to serve.

Tip... Make sure that if you are using a frying pan for this
recipe it has a metal or ovenproof handle, otherwise use a
round cake tin.

Variations... Use other vegetables, such as de-seeded, diced
red or green peppers or cubes of aubergine, in place of any
of those used here.

If you like, replace the olive oil with calorie controlled
cooking spray. Spray the vegetables on the baking tray in
step 2.

Stuffed courgettes

Serves 2
185 calories per serving
Takes 15 minutes to prepare,
30–40 minutes to cook
ⓥ

15 g (½ oz) sun-dried
tomatoes
¼ **kettleful of boiling water**
2 small courgettes, halved
lengthways
40 g (1½ oz) ciabatta
breadcrumbs (see Tip)
1 teaspoon dried oregano
1 garlic clove, crushed
1 tablespoon pine nut kernels
15 g (½ oz) low fat spread
calorie controlled cooking
spray
salt and freshly ground black
pepper
a handful of fresh basil leaves,
to garnish

*Small courgettes are best for this dish as they tend to be
sweeter and look nice too.*

1 Preheat the oven to Gas Mark 5/190°C/fan oven 170°C.
Place the sun-dried tomatoes in a small bowl, cover with
boiling water and leave to soak for 5 minutes. Drain, reserving
6 tablespoons of the liquid and cut the tomatoes into thin
strips.

2 Using a teaspoon, scoop the middle seeds from the courgette
halves, discard and place the halves in a snug fitting ovenproof
dish. Season the courgettes.

3 Mix together the tomatoes, ciabatta breadcrumbs, oregano,
garlic, pine nut kernels and low fat spread. Season lightly.
Divide the mixture between the courgettes and spray with
the cooking spray. Pour the reserved tomato liquid around the
courgettes. Bake for 30–40 minutes until the courgettes are
just tender and the topping is golden. Garnish with the basil
leaves before serving.

Tip... For the ciabatta breadcrumbs, using a food processor
or hand held blender, whizz the ciabatta until crumbs
form. Alternatively, you can use the equivalent weight in
wholemeal breadcrumbs.

Carrot and butter bean terrine

Serves 4

236 calories per serving

Takes 45 minutes to prepare,
1 hour to cook

Ⓥ

❄

700 g (1 lb 9 oz) carrots,
peeled and diced

1 onion, chopped

1 garlic clove, crushed

600 ml (20 fl oz) vegetable
stock

1 teaspoon ground coriander

2 large eggs

25 g (1 oz) fresh white or
wholemeal breadcrumbs

420 g can butter beans,
drained and rinsed

150 g (5½ oz) low fat soft
cheese with garlic and herbs

salt and freshly ground black
pepper

*This colourful terrine is delicious eaten hot or cold. Serve
with a simple sliced tomato salad drizzled with balsamic
vinegar.*

1 Place the carrots, onion, garlic and stock in a large lidded
saucepan and bring to the boil. Add the ground coriander and
seasoning. Cover and simmer for 15 minutes until the carrots
are tender. Drain well and mash thoroughly or blend in a food
processor. Beat in the eggs and stir in the breadcrumbs.

2 Line a 900 g (2 lb) loaf tin with non stick baking parchment.
Spoon half the mixture into the tin.

3 Mash the butter beans with the soft cheese or blend them
together in a food processor or using a hand held blender.
Spread this over the carrot mixture in the tin. Top with the
remaining carrot mixture.

4 Cover the terrine with a sheet of non stick baking parchment
and then cover the whole tin with foil. Place the tin in a large
saucepan or wok and pour in enough water to come half way
up the sides of the tin. Bring the water to the boil, cover and
reduce the heat. Alternatively, place the tin in a roasting tray
with water and bake at Gas Mark 5/190°C/fan oven 170°C.
Simmer gently for 1 hour. Check the water level from time to
time and top up with boiling water if necessary.

5 Carefully lift the tin out of the water, remove the foil and
baking parchment and let it cool. Run a round bladed knife
around the edge of the terrine to loosen the edges. Place a
serving platter on top of the tin and then turn the tin upside
down so that the terrine drops out on to the platter. Cut it into
eight slices and serve two slices per person.

Spring vegetables with crusty polenta

Serves 4

397 calories per serving

Takes 10 minutes to prepare
+ 1 hour cooling, 20 minutes
to cook

Ⓥ

200 g (7 oz) dried polenta

3–4 fresh sage leaves,
chopped

calorie controlled cooking
spray

salt and freshly ground black
pepper

a few fresh thyme leaves, to
garnish

For the vegetables

8 baby leeks or spring onions,
halved lengthways

200 g (7 oz) small young
asparagus spears

200 g (7 oz) mushrooms,
preferably wild

2 tablespoons balsamic
vinegar

150 ml (5 fl oz) vegetable
stock

Quick cook 'instant' polenta is very easy to prepare and makes a welcome change from potatoes, rice and pasta.

1 Make up the polenta according to the packet instructions. Season and stir in the chopped sage. Line a shallow dish or baking tray with cling film, pour in the polenta and leave to cool and set for at least 1 hour.

2 Preheat the grill or a griddle pan to high and spray with the cooking spray. Turn out the set polenta and cut into 4 or 8 thin slices. Grill for 4 minutes on each side until crusty.

3 Meanwhile, heat a wok or large non stick frying pan over a high heat and spray with the cooking spray. Stir fry all the vegetables for 4–5 minutes until turning brown at the edges. Season, pour in the vinegar and stir fry for 1 minute. Add the stock and boil vigorously for 2 minutes.

4 Place the grilled polenta on four serving plates, spoon the vegetables over, scatter with the thyme leaves and serve.

Tip... Wild mushrooms can be found in the fresh vegetable section of most supermarkets and in delicatessans.

Cauliflower cheese soufflé

Serves 4

270 calories per serving

Takes 15 minutes to prepare,
  50 minutes to cook

Ⓥ

1 small cauliflower, cut into
  florets
calorie controlled cooking
  spray
1 tablespoon fresh
  breadcrumbs
40 g (1½ oz) low fat spread
40 g (1½ oz) plain flour
425 ml (15 fl oz) skimmed milk
3 egg yolks
a pinch of freshly ground
  nutmeg
1 teaspoon French mustard
50 g (1¾ oz) mature Cheddar
  cheese, grated
4 egg whites
salt and freshly ground black
  pepper

*This recipe is a little more involved than the traditional
family favourite cauliflower cheese, but it is really quite
easy and the results are sensational.*

1 Bring a large saucepan of water to the boil, add the
cauliflower and cook for 10 minutes until quite soft. Drain
thoroughly and then mash.

2 Meanwhile, preheat the oven to Gas Mark 6/200°C/fan
oven 180°C and prepare an 18 cm (7 inch) soufflé dish by
spraying it with the cooking spray and dusting the sides with
the breadcrumbs.

3 Melt the low fat spread in a small saucepan and stir in the
flour. Add the milk a little at a time, stirring well between each
addition to make a smooth sauce.

4 Remove the sauce from the heat and stir in the egg yolks,
nutmeg, mustard, cauliflower and all but a little of the grated
cheese. Season.

5 In a clean, grease-free bowl, whisk the egg whites until they
form stiff peaks and then gently fold into the sauce. Pour into
the prepared soufflé dish, sprinkle the remaining cheese over
the top and bake for 35–40 minutes, until well risen. Serve
immediately.

Paella with roasted vegetables

Serves 2

381 calories per serving

Takes 5 minutes to prepare,
1 hour to cook

Ⓥ

❄ (rice only)

**calorie controlled cooking
spray**

2 garlic cloves, chopped

**1 teaspoon smoked or regular
paprika**

**a pinch of saffron or
1 teaspoon turmeric**

150 g (5½ oz) dried paella rice

**550 ml (19 fl oz) vegetable
stock**

For the roasted vegetables

2 teaspoons balsamic vinegar

1 tablespoon light soy sauce

**1 red pepper, de-seeded and
quartered**

1 fennel bulb, cut into wedges

2 red onions, cut into wedges

6 asparagus spears

**salt and freshly ground black
pepper**

*Paella usually contains a mixture of meat and seafood, but
this is a tasty vegetable version.*

1 Preheat the oven to Gas Mark 6/200°C/fan oven 180°C.

2 For the roasted vegetables, mix together the balsamic
vinegar and light soy sauce in a bowl and season. Put all the
vegetables in the bowl and turn to coat them in the marinade.

3 Spray a baking tray with the cooking spray and arrange the
vegetables, with the exception of the asparagus, on the tray in
an even layer. Roast for 20 minutes, add the asparagus, turn
the vegetables and cook for another 10–15 minutes.

4 While the vegetables are roasting, spray a non stick frying
pan with the cooking spray and fry the garlic for 1 minute,
adding a splash of water if it starts to stick. Stir in the spices
and rice. Turn to coat the rice in the spices. After 1 minute, pour
in the stock and stir gently so the rice forms an even layer in
the pan.

5 Leave the rice to simmer over a low heat for 30 minutes,
without stirring for the first 20 minutes. As the stock is absorbed,
gently stir the rice occasionally.

6 Serve the rice topped with the roasted vegetables.

Quorn and nut roast with tomato sauce

Serves 6
215 calories per serving
Takes 25 minutes to prepare,
   30 minutes to cook

Ⓥ
❄

calorie controlled cooking
   spray
1 large onion, chopped
1 garlic clove, crushed
300 g (10½ oz) Quorn mince
110 g (4 oz) fresh brown
   breadcrumbs
60 g (2 oz) mixed chopped
   nuts
1 tablespoon dried mixed
   herbs
1 tablespoon yeast extract
1 egg, beaten
2 tomatoes, sliced
2 teaspoons poppy seeds

For the sauce
400 g can chopped tomatoes
½ vegetable stock cube,
   crumbled
1 tablespoon tomato purée

This can be made ahead and frozen.

1 Preheat the oven to Gas Mark 4/180°C/fan oven 160°C.
Line a 900 g (2 lb) loaf tin with non stick baking parchment.

2 Spray a small non stick frying pan with the cooking spray,
add the onion and cook for 10 minutes over a low heat until
softened. Add the garlic and cook for a further minute.

3 Place the Quorn, breadcrumbs, nuts and herbs in a large
bowl, mix well and stir in the onion and garlic. Dissolve the
yeast extract in 2 tablespoons of hot water and add with the
egg. Mix to a thick batter consistency with 300 ml (10 fl oz)
of water.

4 Spoon half the mixture into the tin, top with the tomato slices
and then add the remaining mixture. Sprinkle with the poppy
seeds and bake for 30 minutes until brown on the top and set.

5 For the sauce, place the ingredients in a small pan, bring
to the boil and simmer for 2–3 minutes until hot and slightly
thickened. Serve the nut roast sliced, with the sauce drizzled
over.

Cabbage parcels

Serves 4

232 calories per serving

Takes 40 minutes to prepare,
35 minutes to cook

Ⓥ

1 large Savoy cabbage, leaves
removed carefully to keep
them whole and then washed

100 ml (3½ fl oz) white wine

400 g can chopped tomatoes

1 garlic clove, chopped finely

a small bunch of fresh basil,
chopped roughly, to garnish

For the stuffing

30 g (1¼ oz) sun-dried
tomatoes

a kettleful of boiling water

8 porcini mushrooms

100 g (3½ oz) dried couscous

2 tablespoons toasted pine nut
kernels

a small bunch of fresh parsley,
chopped

a small bunch of fresh mint,
chopped

grated zest and juice of a
lemon

salt and freshly ground black
pepper

*Based on the Greek recipe for stuffed vine leaves called
dolmathes, this has been adapted to use Savoy cabbage
leaves, which have the advantage of being larger to allow
more filling.*

1 Bring a large saucepan of water to the boil, add the cabbage
leaves and blanch for 5 seconds. Drain and refresh with cold
water. Cut any large leaves in half by cutting out the middle
stem.

2 Preheat the oven to Gas Mark 4/180°C/fan oven 160°C.
Place the sun-dried tomatoes in a small bowl, cover with
boiling water, leave to soak for 5 minutes and then drain and
slice. Place the porcini mushrooms in another small bowl,
cover with boiling water, leave to soak for 5 minutes and then
drain and chop.

3 Meanwhile, put the couscous in a bowl and pour over
enough boiling water to cover it with 2.5 cm (1 inch) to spare.
Cover with a plate, foil or a clean tea towel and leave to steam
for 5 minutes.

4 Mix all the stuffing ingredients together in a bowl.

5 Fill the leaves by placing 1 tablespoon of the stuffing at the
stalk end of the leaf and rolling once before folding in the sides
and continuing to roll. Secure with cocktail sticks and put in an
ovenproof dish. When one layer is complete, season and then
start another. (The mixture will make about 20 parcels.)

6 Pour over the wine and tomatoes, season, sprinkle over the
garlic and cover with foil before baking for 35 minutes. Scatter
with the basil and serve.

Asparagus and leek tart

Serves 2
238 calories per serving
Takes 25 minutes

Ⓥ

❄

80 g (3 oz) puff pastry
1 large leek, chopped finely
1 tablespoon fresh thyme
** leaves**
1 beaten egg
8 asparagus tips
1 fresh rosemary sprig
calorie controlled cooking
** spray**
salt and freshly ground black
** pepper**

A simple but very pretty tart.

1 Preheat the oven to Gas Mark 6/200°C/fan oven 180°C.
Roll out the pastry into an 8 cm (3¼ inch) square and place
it on a non stick baking tray. Gently push up the edges of the
pastry to make a slight ridge all the way round.

2 Bring a saucepan of water to the boil and steam the leek
for 3 minutes until tender. Squeeze out any excess water and
combine the leek with the thyme.

3 Brush the pastry square with some beaten egg to glaze and
spoon the leek mixture over the top, leaving a 1 cm (½ inch)
gap around the edge. Arrange the asparagus on top of the
leek. Season well, place the rosemary on top and spray with
the cooking spray. Bake for 15 minutes or until the pastry is
cooked and golden.

Index